Finding Time

for the Timeless

Finding Time
for the Timeless

Spirituality in the Workweek

John McQuiston II

Walking Together, Finding the Way
SKYLIGHT PATHS Publishing
Woodstock, Vermont

Finding Time for the Timeless:
Spirituality in the Workweek

2004 First Printing
© 2004 by John McQuiston II

Library of Congress Cataloging-in-Publication Data
McQuiston, John.
Finding time for the timeless : spirituality in the workweek / John McQuiston II.
p. cm.
Includes bibliographical references.
ISBN 1-59473-035-0
1. Spirituality. 2. Spiritual life—Christianity. I. Title.
BV4501.3.M38 2004
248—dc22x

2004015480

10   9   8   7   6   5   4   3   2   1
Manufactured in Canada

SkyLight Paths Publishing is creating a place where people of different spiritual traditions come together for challenge and inspiration, a place where we can help each other understand the mystery that lies at the heart of our existence.

SkyLight Paths sees both believers and seekers as a community that increasingly transcends traditional boundaries of religion and denomination—people wanting to learn from each other, *walking together, finding the way*.

SkyLight Paths, "Walking Together, Finding the Way" and colophon are trademarks of LongHill Partners, Inc., registered in the U.S. Patent and Trademark Office.

Walking Together, Finding the Way
Published by SkyLight Paths Publishing
A Division of LongHill Partners, Inc.
Sunset Farm Offices, Route 4, P.O. Box 237
Woodstock, VT 05091
Tel: (802) 457-4000 Fax: (802) 457-4004
www.skylightpaths.com

CONTENTS

In reality the main purpose of life is to raise everything that is profane to the level of the holy.

—Martin Buber

Lord, hear my prayer. For my days drift away like smoke.

—Psalms 102:1, 3

PREFACE

One morning I received an e-mail from Maura Shaw, who told me she was an editor. She had read a *New York Times* article about men and women who managed to pray during the business day. Maura was looking for someone who would collect similar stories for a book. Phyllis Tickle, a mutual friend, had suggested me. Would I be interested?

I had been suggested because I had written a short book about attempting to incorporate some of the principles of monastic life into my own life as a lawyer. (Keyword: "attempting.") On paper I looked like a good candidate for her project. However, I explained to Maura, although I had written about incorporating prayer into my life, I had only had limited success in doing it. Maura kindly brushed aside this objection (perhaps she had no other candidates), and I agreed to try. I considered that collecting stories about contemporary spiritual practices, particularly those that occur during the workweek, could be a way to renew my own.

Relative to most people in the world, my life and the lives of the people who will read this book are lives of material prosperity. But, as we know, material well-being doesn't guarantee happiness. A recent *Atlantic Monthly* article reported on the results of a multi-cultural study on the relationship between wealth and happiness. The study, conducted by Dutch sociologist Ruut Veenhoven, concludes that an increase in material affluence does produce a substantial increase in "happiness" (whatever that is) for those at the bottom of the economic ladder. But once a fairly minimal level of security is attained, an increase in possessions produces no substantial enhancement in the enjoyment of life.[1] If possessions do not increase happiness, what does?

I believe that some of the things that actually can enhance life are being loved, performing meaningful work, and practicing certain spiritual disciplines. With this in mind, I revised the project Maura had given me. Instead of limiting my inquiry to prayer, at least not to "prayer" as commonly understood, I used Maura's project as a way to search for spiritual practices that appeared to produce a genuinely higher quality of life.

Perhaps all the practices described in this book can be considered forms of prayer, perhaps not. Maura's task raised a number of questions. What is prayer? Is it meditation? Is it closing our eyes and addressing some words to God? Can prayer be wordless? In order to pray, must we believe in a God who is conscious in the same way we are? Can action be a type of prayer? When we help a stranger, or give time or money, is that a kind of prayer? When we read something that speaks to our deepest longings, is that prayer? What is the purpose of prayer? Are some objectives of prayer legitimate and others improper? Prayers for forgiveness, for health, for friendship, for victory, for prosperity, and for love are all prayers seeking something for the person praying. Is that okay?

I am a lawyer. In law school we learned by studying cases. Business schools also use the case-study method. Cases are simply stories. Jesus used stories, such as the good Samaritan and the prodigal son, in his teachings. The tales of the Hasidim, and much of the Bible, are stories from which the reader can draw his or her own (frequently differing) conclusions. So instead of trying to answer these questions about prayer (which I couldn't answer anyway), I have collected these stories.

I have limited myself to recounting the experiences of "ordinary" people, if there is such a thing. By this I mean that I deliberately avoided interviewing anyone who is a priest, rabbi, pastor, or guru. In some cases, for various reasons, details and identities have been changed. Some reports were written without conducting an interview, because I already knew that friend or family member well enough to write about him or her. Thus a few people may be surprised to recognize themselves here. I offer my apologies to them. During the year that I collected these accounts, I also recorded some of my own life. The stories are interspersed with whatever was going on with me at the time.

When this collection of stories was almost finished, I received an e-mail from one of Maura's co-workers asking me to write a few sentences about why someone would read this book. My answer is that these accounts are evidence that it is possible, despite all the contrary pressures of contemporary society, to find the time to bring a more profound dimension into daily life, and to do so even during the workweek. These stories teach that the individuals who have accomplished this do not have to force themselves: Each has found a practice that he or she enjoys.

Paul Tillich, one of the most influential theologians of our time, observed that "in our period of history, work has become the dominating destiny of all.... It has become a religion itself."[2] Although there is no common practice reflected here, every story illustrates a successful defeat, at least for a time, of the prevailing mindset of our culture—the mindset of work and worry.

In collecting these accounts I was not concerned with cataloging beliefs. My focus was on actions and practices. I am sure that the beliefs of the individuals portrayed in this book vary widely, but I am equally sure that each of them has an understanding, either intuitive or express, that in order to bring a spiritual dimension into life, regular actions are crucial, because such actions become habits, and habits (for good or ill) change the quality of one's life.

This book focuses on individuals and individual practices. But everyone described here is connected in some way with a faith community or tradition. Indeed, none of us is as isolated an individual as we may think we are. We think of ourselves as separate creatures, yet a moment's reflection shows that this is an illusion. We are always in relationships with other people, and if those relationships are impaired, so are we. Food, air, and water flow through our bodies, and without them, we die. We are the products of the infinite, impenetrable mystery from which we came; in which we live, move, and have our being; and to which we return. Whether by meditation, religious rituals, contemplative prayer, or acts of service, we acknowledge that we are a part of something greater than ourselves.

I thank each person who is described here for sharing something of his or her life with me. My sketches do not do them justice. In life, as in religion, words are only a suggestion of the reality they purport to describe.

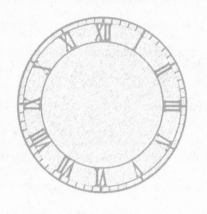

Wondering What Could Change

It is early on a Monday morning. Phillip has been at work for two hours. He is the only person at his company's office. The daylight is just appearing. Phillip is reading the letters, e-mails, and memos that came while he was on a trip the previous week. In a few minutes his co-workers will fill the office.

Phillip is sixty years old. He has a wife and two grown children. His home is paid for. He finished educating his children a few years ago. They both went to graduate school. He is in reasonably good health: not perfect, but good. He is slightly overweight. He has a bad back and moderately high cholesterol. He attends church, but he does not consider himself to be religious.

Phillip has been on the same performance-based track for his entire life. Although he has achieved financial success and considers himself lucky, he feels he has missed something of importance—that indefinable ingredient that could have turned a good life into a fulfilled life. As he sits in his corner office anticipating a busy and productive day, he is not unhappy, but he wonders what he could have done, what he might have learned, or how he should have lived in order to look at his life this morning and say: I am deeply satisfied.

This book is for all of us who sometimes share this feeling with Phillip.

Jason

Wakefulness to God

Jason is the owner-operator of two hamburger fran-
chises in a small city. He does not attend any religious
services of any kind.

Each morning Jason has breakfast while his wife
sleeps. At breakfast he reads. He reads Frederick
Buechner's *Telling the Truth: The Gospel as Tragedy,
Comedy, and Fairy Tale;* the Bible; the Tao Te Ching;
the Bhagavad Gita; the Kabbalah; Martin Buber's *Tales
of the Hasidim;* Raimundo Panikkar's *The Silence of
God: The Answer of the Buddha;* Henry P. Stapp's
Mind, Matter, and Quantum Mechanics; Paul Tillich's
The Dynamics of Faith; Dietrich Bonhoeffer's *Letters*

and Papers from Prison; and so on. For years and years he has read and read.

Jason has tried to meditate, but he cannot if that means being quiet and stilling the mind. However, he points out that the twentieth-century English monk John Main said that "meditation has nothing to do with quiet reverie or passive stillness, but with wakefulness. We awaken to our nearness to God. We realize that the power of creation, the energy of creation, flows in our hearts."[3]

For Jason, mornings with his books are conversations with the authors. He engages their ideas, he underlines, he writes in the margins. Through them, he leaves his usual day-to-day mindset. He says that God is speaking to him through all these voices. They bring him "another way to feel." He reports that during these morning readings he loses the ordinary sense of himself as an isolated individual; he sees himself as a part of a continuum that is infinite in time and depth, a continuum that includes the authors and the rest of the world. Jason says, "The Bible is a collection of books with profound meaning to many people. My personal 'Bible' is also a collection of books—the books that have become a part of my mornings over the years."

Karen
Life as a Prayer

Karen is a photographer for a large daily newspaper. She is Roman Catholic. She has three children. Her day begins at dawn when she lights a candle and listens to music that "keeps me in God's presence." She does some spiritual reading. On her commute, she prays the rosary.

During the day she tries to see God in everything and everyone. She says, "The everything part is easier than the everyone part." She sees her work as a photo-journalist as a calling: "It is who I am, not what I do." Occasionally the newspaper wants pictures of joy or beauty: a small child on Christmas morning or autumn leaves floating on water. More often, her task is to record incidents of pain—accident scenes and buildings destroyed by fire.

Twice a year Karen goes on a three-day retreat. For those three days she immerses herself in prayer and silence. She says, "Aside from attending Mass, this is the single most important practice for maintaining my spiritual life."

Throughout her day, whatever it brings, she reminds herself that she is in the presence of God. She says, "I want my life to be a prayer."

Joe

A Way of Living Every Day

Joe is a physician. An allergist. He is Jewish and he was raised attending Friday night services.

Joe attended a Presbyterian liberal arts college. During his freshman and senior years there, he was required to take courses which surveyed contemporary theologians, mostly Christian and Jewish. Those courses suggested to him the possibility that religion was more than attending services once a week, but for the next fifteen years or so the thought lay fallow.

In his early forties he read two books by Abraham Joshua Heschel: *The Sabbath* and *God in Search of Man: A Philosophy of Judaism*. These books suggested to him what religion could be. He continued to read, but he began to realize that reading wasn't enough, and he also began to pray. Over time he established the routine he now follows.

Joe's daily habit is to pray as soon as he wakes in the morning and again just before going to sleep. Two or three times a week he attends early morning services before going to work. He continues to go to Friday night services, but in recent years he has added attendance at Saturday morning services, which he now often leads.

When asked to compare himself today with the person he was fifteen years ago, he says that his earlier self was completely task-oriented. His life was concentrated on raising a family and making a living. At that time he was absorbed with work, and he prayed only on Friday evenings. He treated the two worlds, the religious and the secular, as if they were completely separate.

Today, however, he cannot separate his religion and his activity in the workweek. For him Judaism is both a way of living and a way of thinking. He feels that in order for religion to be meaningful, it must be lived. As he treats patients, particularly in the more difficult cases, he often thinks, What would God want me to do?

Joe says that you can't exercise for ten minutes a week and stay healthy, nor can you eat a healthy diet one day a week and an unhealthy diet the other six. He feels that religion is the same. He has made every effort to incorporate that way of thinking and doing into all seven days of the week.

There is one difference in his treatment of the Sabbath from the other six days of the week. He feels strongly that the Sabbath day is a gift: a day in which "you can rebel against the secular world. It is a day to put aside work and commerce, and savor time."

Remember the sabbath day, to keep it holy.

—Exodus 20:8

Ana

Music as Prayer

Ana works in a bookstore in one of our largest cities. She has a great sense of humor, but that is not our interest here. "On the side" (from an economic point of view only) she composes, teaches, and performs music. For her, making music is a form of prayer.

About five mornings and evenings a week (she doesn't think it helps to force an activity every day, or to have a rigid schedule) she sings Hindu mantras for about forty minutes. She commutes by train, and she frequently misses the early train. When this happens she sits in her car, watches the river, and sings until the next train is due.

On her commute she sometimes stands between the cars, where she won't disturb anyone, and sings. Because of the noise of the train, when she sings between the cars she wears earplugs. She says the resulting sound is interesting. In her seat on the train she hums to herself. She has a friend who often sits beside her who knows what she is doing. When she gets too loud her friend will poke her and say, "Music leaking."

She uses the beads of a rosary to count the repetitions of the mantra she sings. She points out that in Hindi there are 108 names for God—half that is fifty-four, which is the number of beads on a Catholic rosary. During her work day she hums the notes of mantras that she sings in the morning and the evening.

Ana has a Tibetan "singing bowl" that she purchased at a religious bookstore. It is supposedly made of "the seven precious metals," whatever they are, but she doubts this is true. It was expensive, but cost less than many color televisions. She tested several bowls before she chose one that was right for her. She rubs the rim of the bowl with a stick the store also supplied, and it produces a low, quiet hum on a single note. If she hits the bowl on the rim it produces a bell-like peal. She can change the notes with different water levels in the bowl.

Ana says, "Everything that exists: sounds, light, touches, smells, even the earth itself, is vibration. Our bodies are music boxes, and thus we can change ourselves by changing the patterns of energy—the vibrations—that course through us. This is why music is so powerful, and why music is prayer. It links us to the source of all vibrations."

Breathing into Spirit

Payne is a physician in Oregon. He was born in Mississippi and grew up in Alabama. During college he spent his junior year in Germany at the University of Heidelberg. He was a member of a small Baptist church when he was a teenager, but he is now a Buddhist. He has two sons. One attends college in New York. The other lives with him and attends high school. Although he is divorced, he and his ex-wife are on good terms. His youngest son lived with his mother until it was time to go to high school, and then moved in with Payne because the high school that served Payne's neighborhood was better than the one that served his mother's neighborhood.

Every morning Payne starts his day with an hour of meditation. He wakes about 5:00 a.m. He stretches, using yoga positions to limber his joints. He has a practiced series of movements that he repeats each morning. Then he sits in the traditional cross-legged pose and stills his mind. The best meditations, he says, are those in which he loses his sense of himself.

During the day he tries to practice mindfulness and compassion. Sometimes he finds a place to sit alone and stills himself in order to return to that same state that he reached in meditation or, if that is not completely possible, to as close to that state as he can. He shuts the door to his office, unplugs the cord to the telephone, closes his eyes, and breathes slowly and deeply for a few minutes.

In the evenings he again practices meditation. He has been engaged in daily meditation practice for over thirty years.

When you are in Payne's presence you cannot imagine him being tense. Payne is not particularly concerned with traditional achievement. He is anything but a financial success. But Payne exudes calmness and serenity, and he is as content as anyone I know.

Friendship as Prayer

Helen is an administrator for a local charity. She recruits and assigns duties to volunteers. She schedules their activities and is part of the small team that leads the organization.

She has two daughters, a husband who is a lawyer, and two dogs. She talks to her daughters by telephone several times a week and sees each of them at least once a week. She has been married thirty-seven years.

She speaks on the phone to her friend Ann almost every day and to her friend Susan frequently. Her friendship with Ann began in kindergarten, and her friendship with Susan extends from high school. She also maintains close friendships and weekly contact with Liz and Stephanie. She has been a close friend of Liz since college and of Stephanie since grammar school.

Many believe that we experience God through interpersonal relationships. Is Helen's practice of maintaining these lifelong relationships with husband, daughters, and friends a prayer?

What is your intention?

Friendship.

What do you want from me?

Grace.

—Rumi

Murray
Discovering What You're Looking For

Murray is dead now, but twenty-five years ago he was a parish priest at our Episcopal church. I had read about something called "spiritual direction," and I asked him if he would "direct" me. He agreed to meet with me, although he didn't refer to it as spiritual direction. It was up to me how often we met. We settled on 8:00 a.m. one day a week for about thirty minutes. We met for about a year.

At the time, I was in my late thirties. I had a wife, two daughters, a mortgage, two dogs, and two cats. I was relatively successful in my profession, and everyone in our family was in good health and reasonably happy. Despite all this, I felt that something was missing.

In the mornings Murray and I talked about my life and my feelings. I don't remember asking him about his life or family, but I did learn a lot about Murray over those months even though the topic of conversation, almost exclusively, was me.

Murray was a quietly joyful person. I don't know where it came from, whether it was from his genes, his family, his age (at the time he was in his late fifties), his religious beliefs, or the way he practiced his religion, but he had a happy serenity. He was a small man in stature, a student of theology, an avid reader, an innovative thinker, and somewhat of an introvert. In our conversations he was warm and non-judgmental. During those sessions I had the feeling that he was delighted to be with me, and his only interest was in helping me discover whatever it was that I was looking for.

Murray told me that he read the daily service of morning prayer every morning, and that he had been doing this for decades. So I began to do so. Prior to that time, I had had no daily spiritual practice. Although I no longer read the service of morning prayer each day, for the twenty-five years since Murray gave me the idea, every morning (with only a few exceptions), I have begun my day with some spiritually oriented reading.

Anna Mae
Finding Spiritual Strength

Anna Mae died thirty years ago, but I knew her well. She was the daughter of a prominent Presbyterian minister. Her father graduated from Union Theological Seminary and founded several churches in the South.

She married a cotton farmer and lived out her adult life in a small town in the South. Her husband was unfaithful and they divorced. Because her husband was also a spendthrift, she was left with little to live on. She taught piano. She raised three daughters on very little income.

In her religious practice Anna Mae followed a traditional path. Each day began with Bible reading and prayer. She read through the Bible many times. She attended Wednesday night church suppers and the women's Bible study group. She set the record for consecutive Sunday service attendance at her local Presbyterian church.

She committed large portions of the Bible to memory. She saw to it that her children and grandchildren also committed psalms and Bible verses to memory. When she did her daily Bible readings she felt that she had entered into a sacred space. The Bible for her was a place of mental refuge where she found solace and spiritual strength.

Mohammed Jamil

Unbroken Communication with God

Mohammed Jamil is a Muslim, the father of six children, and a vascular surgeon. He is in his late fifties. I had heard that Muslims are required to pray five times a day, and I asked Jamil if he, as a busy surgeon, was able to do this. Before answering that question he told me that it was basic to his faith that he was never not in touch with God. During our conversation he made the point several times that "our line of communication with God is continuous." In contrast to the stereotypical surgeon who credits himself for good results, he says, "It is the power of God that heals the tissue.

Through God's power, in six months there will be no trace of the surgery I performed this morning."

Jamil tries to perform the required five prayers a day, but during surgery there are times when he cannot. When he cannot pray at the prescribed times, he catches up later in the day. Sometimes he cannot complete the required prayers until the evening.

Most evenings he goes to late evening prayer at his mosque at 8:00 p.m. There he performs the last of the five daily prayers. At the mosque they also engage in Islamic studies.

I asked if, like Christians and Jews, Muslims have a Sabbath day. Jamil explained that on Friday he attends congregational prayers, but Friday is also a workday. He says that there is no equivalent to the Sabbath day.

Before we parted, Jamil reemphasized that during the work day he feels he is in unbroken communication with God. He says that each year he has found God more and more in everything that he does: "There is no separation. There is no special day."

Lisa

Deepening the Experience of Life

Lisa is an anthropologist in her early forties. She lives in the Northeast. She was raised a Roman Catholic but drifted away from the church and stayed away for many years.

As an anthropologist she found herself drawn to studying religious practices, particularly those of Native Americans. Years ago she spent time on an Indian reservation in South Dakota. She was invited to participate in the rituals. Although she was there as an anthropologist, she found herself intrigued at a personal level.

In her mid-thirties she began to make a few random

visits to Catholic churches. She works in a large city, and from time to time she would wander into a sanctuary and sit. In one church she picked up a pamphlet telling her about the activities of the John Main Society and the related World Community of Christian Meditation.

She was immediately interested, and she contacted the society. She did some reading and went to some meetings. She adopted the recommended twenty to thirty minutes of meditation at the beginning and end of the day. Now she realizes that throughout the years in which she had no religious or spiritual practice, she had felt a void. She was looking for a practice that would fulfill her spiritual side, and meditation did this.

She has found that the two times a day of quiet meditation, once in the morning and once late in the evening just before going to bed, keep her rooted, deepen her life experience, and give her a way to experience God. Meditation has also brought her back to the church. The meditation she practices is based on the Benedictine tradition. Lisa reports it has made this religious tradition meaningful to her in an experiential way.

She has now been engaged in the daily practice of meditation for six years. She attributes to it a deepening of her experience of life, and an improvement in her professional life by helping her to be less stressed.

A Monday Morning in January

The green numerals on the clock radio tell me it is 4:55 a.m. Winter. The sun hasn't come up. My wife is asleep. She makes that small sound that is a snore, although the word seems too strong to describe it. She didn't believe me when I first told her she snores. Over the years she has stopped debating the point, but I'm not sure she believes me.

On the floor on my side of the bed there is a chocolate Labrador retriever named Walter. He snores, too. On the floor on the other side of the bed there is a golden retriever named Hannah. She is the only one in this room who sleeps quietly. I am the only one awake.

There is that Monday-morning sense of dismay: in a few hours I will have to go back to work. The weekend is over. It's too early to get up. Do I want to go back to sleep, or search for God? I want to do both.

I lie on my back, breathing slowly, eyes closed and covered with my second pillow. I think about each breath. I breathe deeply.

After a while I imagine myself floating up, through the roof, and past the treetops.

I imagine myself gliding over the earth on a magic carpet. In my mind's eye I jump across the universe. I can go anywhere. I return to the earth's sky. I breathe slowly. I am weightless and colorless. I dissipate into the sky. I am the sky. God is the sky. I breathe the sky. Breathing slowly. Drifting.

From a bottomless place inside, which I can't see— another dimension—there is a wellspring pouring me out into the world. God unfolding me—creating me. God filling me. God behind my eyes. God breathing me. God surrounding me. I rest in the Presence.

Hours later I realize that I had drifted back into sleep.

There is a famous verse that is translated by the King James Version as "And God said to Moses: I am that I am." Martin Buber says that the correct translation of this verse from the Hebrew is "I will be present."[4]

Dan

Connecting with Something Greater

Dan is a trial lawyer with a large law firm. He is a tall man with a good sense of humor and a frequent smile. He is thoughtful about what he says. In trial he is careful to shape his presentations of his clients' cases around what he refers to as the "bedrock" of each case: that is, those facts he will be able to prove. As a result, judges and juries like him and trust him.

Dan was raised in the Roman Catholic Church, but he says he is not a practicing Catholic. He says he has real problems with the creed, and, even before its recent troubles, he had problems with the Catholic

Church as an organization. Despite these reservations, most workdays he attends the 7:30 a.m. Mass at a downtown church near his office.

For Dan the repetition of familiar prayers and participation in the ritual of Holy Communion each day is a way to connect with a "continuum." Dan thinks of the many people who have participated in these same prayers and rituals over the centuries and who are participating in them today. He says that even though he cannot accept a literal interpretation of the creed as true, he can accept the words of the service as an honest effort to connect with something greater. The services remind him that there is something more to each day than the tasks that await him when he reaches the office.

Bhaskar
Prayer as a Constant in Life

Bhaskar is a pediatric surgeon specializing in child-hood cancer. He is Hindu. He is married and has two grown children. He was born in India but moved to the United States in his teens.

Since he was a child he has prayed when he awakes and again in the evening. On a typical day he awakes about 6:00 a.m. He showers, then stops for a few moments to pray in front of a personal altar. Immediately upon his return from work, he showers again and then prays again. During the workweek he prays alone. On weekends he prays with his wife and, if they are present, other family members.

I asked Bhaskar how prayer has shaped his life. He did not understand the question. With some difficulty I asked it several different ways. Finally he said he did not know what effect prayer had had on his life, because there was no time in his life when he did not pray. There was no way to imagine the kind of person he would have been without prayer.

Jennie

Opening Up the World

Jennie is a judge. She is also the mother of six and the wife of a Presbyterian pastor. She was raised a Presbyterian.

About twelve years ago a number of things happened that led her to the Roman Catholic Church. She had long realized that something was missing from her spiritual life. The change started when her husband invited a Roman Catholic priest to speak to their congregation. The priest talked about the Christian and Eastern mystical traditions. It struck her that he talked about people who had experiences "of" God, not merely "about" God.

Later that year, while in Chicago, she wandered into a Catholic bookstore. She purchased a book by Thomas Merton, one by Evelyn Underhill, and a translation of Teresa of Avila's *Way of Perfection*. Saint Teresa's book struck a profound chord with her.

During the ensuing years she has been on a voyage of discovery. It has led her to become an oblate of a Catholic abbey, to become a member of the Roman Catholic Church, and to receive a master's degree in Catholic thought and life.

During the first few years of her movement into the Catholic tradition, she saw herself primarily as a student trying to learn as much as possible. Now, she feels that she is trying to live what she has learned. As a part of that effort she attends Mass at 6:30 a.m. every weekday before going to work.

While it has been difficult at times for her husband to understand her embrace of the Catholic tradition, throughout her journey he has been supportive of her need for the gifts which that tradition has provided to her.

I asked her to contrast her present spiritual life with her life twelve years ago. She says that the difference is night and day—that her whole world has been changed, "opened up." She reports that spiritual discipline changed her way of looking at the world. She does not suggest that there is a uniquely Catholic way to look at the world, or that it is superior. However, she feels that, for her, embracing the Catholic faith has allowed her to experience the world as prayer: to see all of the world as the unfolding of a divine purpose. Although she realizes that the world is a place of pain and suffering, she says that embracing a contemplative life makes it possible to absorb that pain and suffering in a different, deeper way.

Ted
A Happy Routine

Ted is fifty-five. He is a graduate of Brown University and has an advanced degree from Yale. He spent most of his working life with a large company with offices across the country. His job required him to move periodically. He has lived in the Midwest and in the South. Twice divorced, he has a teen-age son who lives with his mother in another city. At the time of his second divorce he became convinced that his career with his long-time employer was going nowhere. He looked for, and found, a job in the city where his aging parents live.

Ted has a very fine voice and an ear for music. He says he would have made a good cantor if he had happened to be Jewish, but he is Methodist. He plays the piano and the guitar. He sings in the choir and sometimes solos.

Ted's days usually include music and meditation. In the morning while he showers, shaves, and breakfasts he listens to the music of classical composers: Schumann, Mozart, Chopin, Ravel, Liszt, Handel, Strauss, Verdi, Berlioz, Vivaldi, Bach, Mendelssohn, and so on. In his car driving to work he sings along, usually to opera.

Ted's office is in a business complex off the expressway that rims his city. There is nowhere to eat within walking distance, so his co-workers either eat in the company lunchroom or get in their cars to go to lunch. Ted has found a convenience store and gas station that sells a variety of luncheon items. He often stops there, picks up a light lunch, and drives to a nearby park. Lunch takes him about ten minutes. He uses the remaining time to meditate.

Two decades ago he attended a retreat in North Carolina. It was there he was introduced to meditation, but he didn't begin to meditate during the workday until a few years ago. He says his meditation routine varies. At times he just sits and asks nothing of himself. Other times he closes his eyes and focuses on his breath. He does not play music when he meditates. Sometimes he uses the Jesus prayer: "Lord Jesus Christ, have mercy on me, a sinner." He feels refreshed after his daily meditation break, and he returns to work feeling as if he has had a nap.

He is dating Susan, who is also divorced. Frequently Susan joins him in meditation. He has a screened-in porch at the rear of his house. He has a CD player on the porch, and in the evenings, if the weather allows, he sits on the porch with his music. He reads and listens.

In the mornings he likes his music to have force. In the evenings he listens to tranquil jazz and quieter classical pieces featuring piano, flute, violin, or cello.

He rarely turns on the television. He says the last year has been the best year of his life. His job, as a mid-level executive with a hospital supply company, is going well. His relationship with his son is as good as possible given the fact that they live in different cities. He and Susan do not plan to marry, but they have become a couple, and they support one another well.

Ted believes that if he had established years ago what he calls his present "happy routine," his entire life would have been different.

Walking toward God

Alice is a classic yuppie: a young, upwardly mobile, urban professional. Alice lives in Minnesota. She travels often. Wherever she is, at home or on the road, she finds places to walk. She has taken long walks along the rim of the Grand Canyon, in the Smoky Mountains, at the Point Reyes seashore, on Mount Desert Island, in the Rocky Mountain National Park, in the English Lake District, in Venice, and at the Vietnam Veterans Memorial. But the majority of her walks are in more mundane places: on farm roads, in small parks, along streams, and on city streets.

Alice has school-age children and a profession. She

tries to walk every day, but she usually succeeds only once or twice during the workweek. On Saturday and Sunday she always walks. When she is traveling on business she finds it easier to find time for her walks. As she walks, she slows her pace of thought. That's it, nothing more: no rigorous discipline, no structured context, no objective beyond the walks themselves.

The contemporary Protestant theologian Brian Taylor says that "being present in the moment is a way of being present to God, who is this very moment."[5]

Sam
Dogs, Fish, Stress, and Prayer

Sam is retired now. He was chief executive officer and co-owner of a multi-state warehousing company. When Sam and a partner purchased the company, they did so in a leveraged buyout that put them deeply into personal debt. Shortly after they acquired the company, interest rates went through the roof, and there was a recession in the industry the warehouses served. It was a time of extreme pressure. At that time Sam began to start each working day with a thirty-minute walk in a nearby park, accompanied by his yellow Labrador retriever. This became his time for prayer.

When things got really tough, Sam would leave the

office around 5:00 p.m. and drive to a nearby fishing lake. He would push out into the lake in a small boat with a trolling motor. He said that while fishing alone, he felt closer to God than in any other place. Two hours of fishing seemed like a week's vacation. One time Sam took his partner with him, but his partner talked business while they fished. That was the last time Sam took anyone with him.

Today, in retirement, the financial pressures are gone. But he has kept up the habit of his walking prayer times.

Rada
Reaching Out to Others

Rada is a Hindu. She came to the United States from India at the age of sixteen to be married to a physician. Her marriage was arranged by her parents. The Indian community in which she was raised was permeated with Hindu religion and culture, and it has always been a part of her life. She had no formal religious education, but, looking back, she says her religion was simply imbued in her. Over the years she and her husband fell deeply in love. In mid-life they were the founders of a Hindu temple in their community in the United States. Just before the dedication of the temple her husband died of a heart attack.

Rada's friend Gloria, who is Jewish, is the person who told me to interview Rada. Both speak of the other in glowing terms, and are more comfortable praising the other than talking about themselves. Rada has participated in worship services at Gloria's temple at Passover, and Gloria has attended services at the Hindu temple.

Since young adulthood Rada has prayed each morning immediately after bathing. In each home in which she and her husband lived, they established an altar as a place of prayer. She feels it is important to have a sacred space in the home.

Her morning routine always includes prayer, and sometimes includes some spiritual reading. She also prays at the temple. She believes it adds an important dimension to pray in community. At her temple there are services at 8:00 a.m., noon, and 5:00 p.m. Frequently she attends the noon service, although she says that she is not primarily oriented toward ritual. She feels she expresses her religion less in terms of ritual and more by personal commitment to a way of life: a commitment to trying to be and do good and, when she fails, to do better tomorrow. She says it is more important how she acts than how many services she attends.

Rada does not use a mantra, and she doesn't consider herself a student of religion. She is a follower of Gandhi, who inspires her to "be the change in the world, so that the world can be as you would want it to be."

If given a choice between taking time for prayer and doing something to help another person, Rada elects to help. She says that Swami Ramakrishna taught that duty is the highest form of worship.

Starting the Day with Quiet

Bill wakes every morning at about 5:00 a.m. He travels a good deal. He is often in New York on business. He stays in a moderately priced hotel (moderate for New York) on the Upper East Side. His home in a medium-sized city is a two-story house in an older neighborhood. Bill has a wife and three daughters.

He has a morning routine that he follows at home and on the road. Minutes after he wakes, he goes for a long walk—usually for about forty-five minutes. When he is at home, Luke, the family's black Labrador retriever, goes with him. The walk used to be a run, but in the last few years, back and joint problems have slowed down both dog and man.

Bill loves the early mornings and his routine. It developed into its present shape over a decade, more or less without conscious planning. Initially he started his mornings with a three- or five-mile run, then showered, ate a quick breakfast, and was off to the office. At some point he began to take a few minutes to read the newspaper. Then he replaced the newspaper with a little reading from the stack of books that was always around. He would dip into one of the books for a few minutes while he ate breakfast.

At this period in his life, after his walk and a shower, Bill has coffee and a roll and reads the service of morning prayer from the Episcopal Book of Common Prayer. Sometimes Bill reads the service out loud, sometimes not. At times he does some other spiritually oriented reading. Bill is unsure when he first read the worship service as a part of his morning practice, but after he had been doing it for some months, he noticed that it changed the character of the rest of his day. After the reading comes the highlight of his morning, to which he looks forward as soon as he wakes. He sits, in quiet, with a second cup of coffee, and does nothing.

The soul should rest in God we are told. But how is this done? It is not done by multiplication of tactical ecstasies. God needs neither vigils, fasting, prayer, [nor] forms of mortification. What is it that God needs to accomplish the divine nature, which is repose? God needs nothing more than for us to offer him a quiet heart. An existence of letting go, and letting be....

—Matthew Fox

Margaret
A Daily Life of Service

Margaret is the chief executive officer of a large charity. The charity is funded by contributions from a wide variety of churches, synagogues, temples, individuals, and community groups. It serves approximately sixty thousand people with twenty different social service programs.

Her organization was founded as an interfaith organization, and its directors, employees, and volunteers represent a broad cross-section of religions. Margaret says that their disparate religious beliefs make no difference to the individuals working together. All share in an appreciation of each other and a commitment to the work they are doing.

Margaret is in her mid-fifties and has three grown daughters. Her husband Bill is the subject of the preceding sketch. Margaret has observed how meaningful it has been to Bill to have a daily spiritual discipline, and she has attempted to do so as well. However, no daily discipline of prayer has worked for her.

For some time she was concerned that she was unable to incorporate regular private prayer into her life. Eventually she realized that her work was her prayer life. She spends her day with people in need and people who are serving those needs. She says that being around so many people who are trying to do the right thing brings more spiritual fulfillment into her life than any private prayer.

The Hindu scripture, the Bhagavad Gita, says that there are two paths to spiritual fulfillment. The first is meditation and the second is service to others.

Paul
The Character of a Life

Paul is an independent investment counselor. He spent many years at a national investment banking firm before leaving with two others to form his own investment advisory firm.

Paul is a member of a large Reform Jewish temple. He is an active member. He has served on many committees for his temple. He attends Friday-night services. On Saturdays he participates in a men's study group in which they enjoy arguing about the meaning of various scriptural passages.

Paul did not tell me this, but I know from another source that his annual financial contribution to the temple is far more than those of many who are much wealthier than he.

Because of the nature of his work, Paul spends time each day keeping up with economic and political news. As he does this, he continually thinks of the effect of events on the international Jewish community. You cannot discuss religion with Paul without feeling his intensity. He takes his religion very seriously. But Paul is anything but dour. He is always smiling and laughing.

Paul's wife was raised a conservative, fundamentalist Presbyterian. She has converted to Judaism. Paul's intensity was an advertisement for a way of life she wanted to share.

Paul's religion permeates his entire life. Each day he reads from the Talmud in the morning and in the evening. During the workday he tries to be thoughtful about ethical values and to practice them in his dealings with employees, clients, and partners. At home he and his wife work to create a "house of peace." Paul believes that by infusing every aspect of their life together with Judaism, they have radically changed the character of their lives.

Harriette
Attention That Is Joyfully Engaged

Harriette owns a bookstore that specializes in old books and books about the South. When asked how she incorporates prayer and devotional time into her life, she responds that she reads devotional books and books of prayers in the mornings. She says it is best when the weather allows her to read and pray on her porch. Harriette is a slight woman in her sixties. She has raised a family and now is entranced with her grandchildren. She is empathetic: whether you are sick or simply ask her to help find a rare book, she becomes fully occupied with your needs. She is, like all of us, a person of contradictions. She is cheerful, and yet she is a worrier.

Paul Tillich says that your God is what concerns you ultimately. If so, then "to pray" is to focus on that which concerns you ultimately. Harriette's most meaningful prayer, one might say, is her grandchildren. They are her great joy. She talks to them almost every day by phone. Frequently, they visit her and she visits them.

Her days are peppered with opportunities to bring her focus to two things: connecting with others—perhaps via a book, a note in the mail, or a visit—and her grandchildren.

In the nineteenth century, Russian Orthodox Bishop Ignatii taught, "Without attention there is no prayer." When Harriette's attention is joyfully engaged, is this prayer?

A Sunday Morning in March

*The riddle of the present is the
deepest of all the riddles of time.*

—Paul Tillich

I am sitting in my living room, watching my golden
retriever watch me. Outside my window the sun is melting the morning frost. I am thinking about the ramifi-
cations of the above quotation. These are some of my
thoughts.

I can never be in the past, although the effect of
the past is always with me. I can see its mark on my
body, and I know its effect on my thoughts. Pictures
and sounds and smells and feelings are stored in memory, but I can never return to the past, even to the past
second. I can never be in the future. Although I may

plan for it, imagine it, leave notes to be read in it, desire it, or dread it, I can never be in it.

It is always now. But now is never quite within our grasp. Always we are moving toward a time that is not, leaving behind a time that is no longer. We cannot stop the movement, even for a millisecond. In the deepest, dreamless sleep, we still are carried, on and on. We are always in the present, yet the instant we try to see it, hold it, or understand it, it is gone.

The poet Antonio Machado said of Christ, "All your words were one word: *Wake up.*" Saint Paul wrote to the fledgling church in Rome, "Now it is high time to awaken out of sleep."

If I "wake up," what is it that I see? I am sitting in my living room, watching my golden retriever watch me. Outside my window the sun is melting the morning frost. Here we sit, quietly, rushing into the future that never is, leaving the past irrevocably behind. Nothing can separate us from this unstoppable, endless cosmic mystery.

It holds out a future we will never reach, creates the present out of the past, and presents us with the ungraspable "now." We are carried in a whirlwind, and we are made of it.

Nabil
Creating a Patient Heart

Nabil is a university professor of biology. He is in his early forties and he is a Muslim. He has four children, three sons and a daughter. Nabil was born in Lebanon. He has lived in the United States since 1979.

Nabil performs the required five prayers every day. He prefers to pray in a mosque. Throughout his adult life he has made it a point to live and work near a mosque. Being a college professor has made it easy to work near a mosque because many universities have them on campus.

As the Qur'an requires, Nabil begins his day just before the sun comes up, with the first of the five daily required prayers. I asked Nabil if, in performing the prayers, he also adopts the required postures. He answered quickly that he does, explaining that the performance of the ritualized postures is an important part of the experience. Nabil says that his religious practices shape his entire life, and their effect "has been to make life worth living." The daily prayers and postures bring order and peace to his life.

Nabil feels it is important to participate in interfaith activities, and he has made it a practice to do so. When I interviewed him, Nabil was the president of the local Muslim society and a part-time lecturer at a Presbyterian theological seminary.

During the month of Ramadan, he fasts. I asked him how someone could fast for a month. He said that the required fast is only during daylight hours. When night comes, it is permissible to eat lightly. Nabil says, "Fasting during the month of Ramadan builds self-discipline and character. Toward the end of the month when hunger pains are greatest, you find that you have enormous strength. Strength that you did not imagine existed within you."

Nabil does not feel that his religious practices are an obligation. He thanks them for creating a patient heart and the ability to persevere and to love life.

After the September 11, 2001, attack on the World Trade Center, Nabil, because he was not a U.S. citizen and because he was a Muslim born in Lebanon, was arrested and detained. As a result, he lost his university teaching position. Deportation proceedings were commenced despite the fact that he had lived in the United States for twenty-five years and has four children who are U.S. citizens. He was handcuffed, fingerprinted, photographed, jailed, and scheduled for deportation. His case was aggravated by the fact that his visa had expired. But it had expired while he was waiting for the government to process his renewal application.

At the hearing before an immigration judge, the

large turnout of Nabil's supporters packed the small courtroom beyond its seating capacity. There was testimony from numerous community leaders of his city. Following a ninety-minute hearing, the U.S. immigration judge reinstated his visa and he was allowed to stay.

Although he had lost his job and believed he was about to be separated from his family, Nabil never despaired. He says that was the result of a lifetime of prayer.

True piety is this:

to believe in God, and the Last Day,

the angels, the Book, and the
  Prophets,

to give of one's substance, however
  cherished,

to kinsmen and orphans,

the needy, the traveler, beggars,

and to ransom the slave,

to perform the prayer, to pay the
  alms.

—Qu'ran Sura 2:17

The Gift of Talents

Jim has been a top executive in three companies that are household names. He has three grown children, two daughters and a son. He has two grandchildren. Until her death last year from cancer, he was married to his college sweetheart. He is enormously wealthy. He is a hard worker. He is personable. His sense of humor is always evident. He is the kind of person about whom one says, "He never met a stranger."

Jim has retired from running companies, but he will never retire from business. He sits on a number of corporate boards, and he is an active investor in many enterprises of various sizes and in various stages of growth.

Jim is not contemplative. He doesn't meditate. He does not do yoga. He doesn't spend a lot of time thinking about religious subjects. If you ask him, he will say that he believes in God, but he doesn't take the conversation any further. When his children were teenagers, he taught Sunday school for high-school seniors. His class spent their time talking about ethical decision making, not theology.

Since "retirement," Jim has given away a large part of his considerable fortune. He and his wife made a commitment to give it all away before they die. Before giving to a particular charity or institution or setting up a new means to attack a particular problem, Jim investigates. Just as he did in business—with targets, report dates, supervision, and checks and balances—his practice is to study the problem, consult those who offer possible solutions, decide on a strategy, and then set up a vehicle to accomplish his objective.

For Jim, giving away his money and his business

talent is his way of fulfilling his life. For him, material success is a means to a further goal. Does Jim's story belong in a collection of spiritual case studies? Of prayer? It depends upon your definition.

Herbert

Recognizing the Opportunity

Herbert is in his late eighties. He was an artillery officer in Europe in World War II. He was with the first army company to enter Dachau. He is a lifelong student of comparative religion, and he is a devout Reform Jew.

He is not wealthy, but he could have been. He is a lawyer and his corporate clientele provided him with the means and the contacts to become very well off, but he was never interested. Recently I was told by a family friend of Herbert's that since he returned home from Army service in World War II, he has given away half his income every year.

Two large companies he represented for over fifty

years repeatedly requested, without success, that he increase his billing rate to them. He still lives in the house that he purchased shortly after he returned from the war. Although one of his clients is a large furniture chain, his living room furniture is as old as the house.

Herbert is, like Jim, a giver. No one who has asked Herbert for money for what he considers a true charity has ever been refused. (He does not consider the opera or the symphony to be true charities.) Herbert gives in ways that many of us would not recognize as giving. When he was practicing law he generously compensated employees and always billed clients at a low rate. He says he has spent his life with his clients and his co-workers, and he has gotten more satisfaction from helping clients and employees than he could ever have had from the money.

He walks to the courthouse every Friday, and on his way he is good for a handout to every panhandler who happens to ask. Herbert says, "They do me a favor by providing me the opportunity."

Thinking about Herbert makes me recall the debate in Christianity between whether one is saved by faith or by works. Martin Luther wrote that we are saved by faith, not by works. He even suggested that the Book of James should be removed from the New Testament because it said, in no uncertain terms, "faith without works is dead." But Saint Augustine agreed with Saint James. In the *Enchiridion* Augustine said, "For when we ask how good a person is, we do not ask what they believe or what they hope for, but what they live."

I think that Augustine and James were right. How we live, what we do, is more important than whether we use the "correct" verbal formula to express beliefs. Jesus didn't write any words down. He didn't leave us with a creed. The Roman emperor Constantine insisted, 325 years after Jesus, that the squabbling church leaders agree on a written creed. The most widely used Christian creed, the "Nicene Creed," was the result of a political compromise reached by the Council of Nicea. Instead of a creed Jesus left us with an example—a completely selfless life.

And, while I am on the subject, I think that many Christian theologians have misinterpreted both Saint Paul, who is the original fellow who said we are saved by faith, and Martin Luther. Both said having faith is primary. I think what Paul and Luther meant was that to have faith means to live with an attitude of unfaltering trust: a trust potentially so absolute that one loses concern for self. Having an attitude of "faith," or trust (lack of fear, lack of concern for self), is a very different thing from convincing myself that I believe in a particular set of propositions set forth, for example, in a creed.

If Jim gives all his money during his lifetime, if Herbert has given half of his income away every year of his adult life, they have both faith and works, and a lot more of both than I do.

Nastha
The Kingdom of Love on Earth

Nastha is in her early thirties. She is a Hindu of Indian descent. She is unmarried. She grew up in a traditional Hindu family in a major city in the United States. She was educated at an exclusive private school. She is working on a doctoral degree in molecular biology.

Nastha uses a traditional Hindu mantra, "Rama, Rama, Rama." It is the same mantra that Mahatma Gandhi used, and she has been told that it is a very popular mantra in India. According to Nastha, that mantra is a prayer asking that the kingdom of love be established on earth. She was taught the mantra by her mother, who also gave her a book to read about the life of Gandhi written by Eknath Easwaren. Easwaren was a Hindu philosopher who taught in the United States during the last thirty years of his life.

Nastha prays in the morning when she wakes. She has made a small altar on the top of her chest of drawers. She bathes before she begins her prayer time. She says that the mantra "Rama, Rama, Rama" carried Mahatma Gandhi through his tumultuous life, and she has found that the same mantra works for her. It reminds her not only of her heritage, but also that there is a larger dimension to everything that is occurring in her life.

David

Help, Forgive Me, and Thank You

David is a newspaper columnist who writes about religion. I asked him for an interview, but he said he would prefer to send me an e-mail. This is what he wrote:

"You asked what I do to incorporate a spiritual dimension into my workaday life. My big spiritual breakthrough came when I realized that all of life should be lived in a spiritual dimension.

"I started covering religion ten years ago. At first, I covered it like any other beat, as a curious and somewhat skeptical journalist. I covered the institutions; the big meetings and big events; and big, important people, places, and issues. I covered religion like you would cover government or business.

"It didn't seem right. I felt like I was missing the story. But what else could I do? I was trained to report objectively. Religion can be so subjective. After all, there's no way to confirm anything with God, not even God's existence. So I covered religion as if it were just another big institution.

"That's when I stumbled across a quote from Rabbi Harold Kushner: 'For the religious mind and soul, the issue has never been the existence of God but the importance of God, the difference God makes in the way we live.'

"I made a copy of that quote and taped it to the top of my keyboard. It's still there. I look at it all the time. It reminds me that I am not writing about religion. I am writing about God and the difference God makes in the way we live with and among each other individually and collectively.

"That's why I write a column called 'Faith Matters.' It's not called 'Religion Matters' or 'Church Matters' or 'Christianity Matters.' It's called 'Faith Matters' because I believe faith matters all the time in all we do, not only as adherents of particular faiths but also as citizens, taxpayers, neighbors, co-workers, workers, parents, children, and so on.

"I'm very fortunate. I have a job that not only allows me to incorporate a 'spiritual dimension,' but that requires me to do so.

"Still, it's easy to drift away, to get pushed or pulled away from 'the ground of all being,' as Paul Tillich called it. I do work for a corporation. I do live in a thoroughly secularized culture. So, thanks to my wife and a few very close friends, there are things I do to try to stay grounded, anchored, centered, or whatever image you like.

"Basically, I have three disciplines I try to maintain: prayer, study, and relationship. First, I pray. All the time. I pray at home, at work, in the car, and in meet-ings and interviews. Even in church. I have three basic prayers: Help, Forgive Me, and Thank You. Sometimes I elaborate, other times I don't. Often I pray before and during the time I'm writing a column. Usually, it goes something like this: 'Lord, help me to say what needs to be said.'

"I pray with my eight-year-old son every night. We pray the Lord's Prayer and then run through a 'God bless' list of family and friends. I also pray again before I go to bed for each of my children and my wife.

"Next, I study a lot. Usually, I do that alone. I read a lot. I spend a lot of time with people whom I con-sider spiritual giants or geniuses. Jesus, of course. The Old Testament prophets. To a lesser extent, Buddha and Lao-tzu.

"I'm also a big fan of folks like Nouwen, Bon-hoeffer, Merton, Underhill, Parker Palmer, Kushner,

Brueggemann, Wink, Wendell Berry, Ched Myers, Annie Dillard, Elizabeth O'Connor, Heschel, Coffin, Will Campbell, Ken Carder, Verna Dozier—I could go on.

"I study with others, too. I try to be involved in a community Bible study or a servant leadership class all the time. I've come to believe the Bible should be read and discussed and discerned in community. In community Bible study, the text is read twice out loud. Then we each respond to three questions: What disturbs you about this text? Who in this text do you relate to? What is this text telling you or your community of faith?

"In servant leadership classes, a small group of folks have a common reading on a topic such as call or discipleship. Each week, we write one to two pages in response to a question or two, then meet and read our papers to each other.

"Third, I try to stay in relationship with folks in a community of faith. I'm not talking about a congregation, although I think communal sacramental worship is vital to faith. I'm talking about folks who are trying to live in spiritual community with each other. Folks who are trying to live faithfully, deeply, and self-sacrificially in God. Folks who are holding each other up and holding each other accountable. Folks who not only teach their kids about faith but also learn about faith from their kids. Folks who are in relationship with the poor, not only in ministry to them. I'm not good at it. I'm more of a loner. But thankfully I married someone who is very good at it. When I drift away, she pulls (okay, sometimes drags) me back.

"There you have it. Nothing fancy or quirky or even that interesting. No doubt way more than you wanted to know."

What David did not reveal in the above e-mail is that although he is not wealthy, and although he has three children of his own, he and his wife found two children who needed help and they provided it by taking them into their home and raising them as family.

The Spiritual Commute

Katherine works for an advertising agency. She prays as she drives to work. Can someone pray and drive safely at the same time? She says she can, although she once ran a red light. It must depend upon the type of prayer.

She jokes that prayer is necessary given the way people drive. But she prays something more than "get me to work safely."

Her commute takes twenty minutes. It is her time alone. There is no telephone in her car, and the radio is turned off. She starts with singing. The songs vary: "This is the day that the Lord hath made, let us rejoice and be glad in it," the doxology, some hymns from her childhood that she has modified—"Father, I adore you, lay my life before you, how I love you. Jesus I adore you ... Spirit I adore you...." She sings the Lord's Prayer. She sings "Come Holy Ghost, Creator blessed, and in my heart take up thy rest...." Her windows are up. At stoplights anyone looking at her would think she was talking on a car phone.

After the singing she says the prayer of Saint Francis, and she follows that with affirmations and petitions: "Lord Jesus Christ, Son of God, have mercy on me, a sinner" and "Jesus is my refuge." At the end of the drive she pauses and gives thanks, naming things she is thankful for.

Ray
Inspired by the Psalms

Ray is a freelance writer. He is in his late thirties. He has a wife and children.

When I asked him about his spiritual practices, he said that he writes. "Writing slows you down, particularly if you are going to write poetry. My holy grail is slowing down to the point where you are totally aware—you get under the noise."

In the morning Ray reads a psalm, and then he writes down what he feels about it. "In order to understand what is going on in my life, I have to write. It gives me permission to be creative. Each word has meaning.

You sharpen your powers of observation. You must make every word count. You become mindful. Writing trains your focus."

A Monday in June on a Train in France

We have bad seats: partial window, riding backwards. The day is overcast. We are traveling, my wife and I, with two women from our church, Jeanne and Janet. We are making our way to Taizé, a French monastery, where we will spend a week. We have just spent two days in Paris.

In Paris, Jeanne was always the last: last to get up, last to join us to go to the Louvre, last to check out of our hotel (the taxi had to wait), and the last to get her ticket at the train station. Buying her ticket for this train, Jeanne, who is attractive to men, had a long conversation with the male ticket agent. I was nervous about missing the train. When she joined us, I complained about the time it took her to get her ticket. (It had seemed like hours to me.) I should not have. We had fifteen minutes to spare when we found our seats.

Riding in the train now, I feel guilty about my comments to Jeanne about her tardiness. She is usually last, but she has never made us miss anything. I need to cool it.

As we sit, Janet realizes that she has lost her ticket. She gets up to see if she has dropped it in the car. I get up (reluctantly) to help. She finds it on a seat a few rows back. How she managed to drop it there, we will never know. Perhaps it was on the floor and someone put it there. I say, laughing, "It's like traveling with children." But why do I feel responsible?

Settled, the train moving fast now, and surprisingly quietly, I decide to try to practice the presence of God. I think: God is this moment.

The train is smooth. In the background are low conversations in French, which I do not understand. They are similar to the low hum of the air conditioner in our hotel room last night. Is it necessary (as recommended in the book I have just been reading) to concentrate the breath in order to quiet the mind? I don't find it is.

We are riding through broad, flat, green fields. I do not know what crops we see, perhaps wheat? A cell phone rings; an older lady begins a murmured conversation. The last time my wife and I were on a train it was to go from Memphis to New Orleans, and my cell phone would only work if we were near a town.

God is here, not holy, not gilt-edged, not sanctified by any ritual, just present: the expression of the infinite in its finite garb. No need to do anything, just to be.

Jack
Just Being a Friend

Jack is a retired television executive. He says that he goes to church because he was raised that way, but the prayers during church services do little for him. He has tried to pray privately, but that hasn't been satisfactory either. He says, "When I try to pray, I seem always to be praying for something for me. It doesn't seem right to be praying for something for myself."

About a year and a half ago Jack volunteered to help children in a public school with their homework. He was assigned to help Percy, a ten-year-old fatherless boy from the proverbial wrong side of the tracks. Percy was assigned to Jack because Jack is a large, imposing man, and the women at Percy's school were getting nowhere with him. Percy picked fights. Percy skipped school. It was said that Percy stole from his fellow students.

They started by meeting each Wednesday after school. Things began awkwardly. Jack had trouble deciding how to deal with a young boy who was not a family member, and who had no particular desire to be at these meetings. Percy was suspicious of Jack and resentful that he was required to stay after school. But they kept on.

After a few months had gone by, they had developed a degree of friendship. After a few more months Percy accepted an invitation to go fishing with Jack on a Saturday. More time passed. Percy began to talk to Jack about his life away from school, and to ask Jack's advice. Jack had to rein himself in when his advice was requested, because Jack would change almost everything about Percy's life if he could. So Jack tried to avoid telling Percy what to do and instead tried hard to be a help to Percy by just being a friend.

That school year is behind them, and Percy is no longer required to meet with Jack. But Jack is still meeting with Percy. Percy is not only doing better in school; he seems to be doing better in other ways, too.

Jack doesn't meditate. He doesn't pray much. He has never talked to Percy about religion. I asked Jack what he did for his spiritual well-being. Jack told me about Percy.

Elise

Beyond Time and Money

Elise died three years ago at the age of ninety-four. She was a physician who practiced until she was in her eighties. She was raised in a small Tennessee town in a strict Associate Reformed Presbyterian (ARP) household. She did not drink, play cards, or dance. She married a fellow student whom she met in college, who was also an ARP. After she became a doctor and he became a college English professor, they founded a small ARP church in their large city. She sang in the choir. They had no children. It was her decision that children would take her away from her chosen way of life.

Elise's prayer life was not apparent to those around her. Certainly she prayed the prayers of her denomination on Sundays with the congregation, but as far as one could tell, she did not otherwise pray. Yet she was always at peace, quietly joyful in a way that you only noticed when you stopped to think about it.

Her patients had to be truly patient because she sometimes kept them waiting for hours in a communal waiting room with out-of-date magazines. Yet no one seemed to mind because, when she saw you, you were her total focus—as if she had no one else in the world to see. She smiled when you came into her examining room because she was happy, and she was glad to share her happiness with you. She asked about your family, and she remembered the last report on them that she had had from you, perhaps several years before. There was no hurry, no schedule. Her time was yours. You were her sole concern for as long as you were with her.

If you couldn't pay, that was not a problem. She

accepted payment in fruit and vegetables if that was offered, but she never confronted anyone about a bill. She saw patients for years who had not paid a dime. She took one middle-aged woman named Bert into her home. Bert had had a frontal lobotomy and could not find work, so Elise gave her their extra bedroom. Bert lived there for over twenty years. Her "rent" was providing some limited help around the house.

At Elise's funeral, four of her former patients told me that she had paid their hospital bills. Elise was oblivious to two of the most powerful forces in our culture: time and money. Perhaps she succeeded in making her life a prayer.

A July Morning in Maine

It is 6:45 a.m. on a July morning in Maine. The house is surrounded by fog. Upstairs my wife, my daughter, and my son-in-law are still sleeping. There is just enough drizzling rain to keep me off the golf course. Is this heaven? It should be. Where is my prayer? My joy in being? Instead I have been thinking of all I have to do when I return home.

I think about George every time we come to Maine. George is an Episcopal priest. He is an enthusiastic person. He is almost always "up." He has the gift of good humor. Twenty-five years ago, when we were planning a family trip, he insisted we stay at the Asticou Inn in Northeast Harbor, Maine. He told us we would love it. At some expense, our family flew to Boston and drove five hours to the inn. We stayed a week. When we returned, George asked me how it was. He said he wanted to know because he had never been inside the inn. He had only seen it in passing when he and his wife boarded a ferry boat on their honeymoon. He said this in his usual manner: that is, with a chuckle.

Because we love Maine, we have been back for summer vacations many times since then. Did George worry about sending us on that first trip? I am sure he did not. Does George worry? Does he pray? He is a priest, but I can't visualize him in deep, contemplative prayer.

Thomas Traherne was an English poet and Anglican priest who lived in the 1600s. He wrote: "Your enjoyment of the world is never right, till every morning you awake in Heaven; see yourself in your Father's Palace; and look upon the Skies, the Earth and the Air as Celestial Joys."[6] Is it possible that Traherne was able to enjoy this world as heaven every day? Or most days? Or some? George seems to. And to get to the point I am really interested in: Is it possible for me?

For years our families, George's and mine, were members of a group that went hiking together for a week each spring. But we have gone separate ways. George has divorced and remarried. I remember George joking and laughing. I envy his joie de vivre. Is that what Traherne was recommending?

An obscure saint, Isaac of Nineveh, in a book called *The Art of Prayer,* said, "The ladder that leads to the Kingdom is hidden within you, and is found within your own soul. Dive into yourself and in your soul you will discover the rungs by which to ascend."

I look out the window at the Maine fog, searching for the experience of heaven, and I begin to think of the tasks that wait for me at the office. I realize that being concerned with the past (George) and the future (the office) is not what I need to be doing this morning, particularly on vacation.

As I sit on this porch and search for the rungs on which to ascend, I think—I have been brought to this morning by a process that began billions of years ago; I am an amalgamation of stardust that has miraculously been made aware; I am cradled in the hands of God; I am a part of the living, conscious expression of the Infinite. How can I worry about what I have to do when I return to the office? I will still be a manifestation of the unlimited, holy mystery as much next Monday as today.

Harry
The Energetic Presence of God

Harry is in his mid-thirties. A bachelor. He is a stock-broker. He graduated from the University of Texas and has an MBA from the Kellogg School of Management. He is from Arizona.

Harry wanted to believe in God but could not. A few years ago he read David Bohm's book *Wholeness and the Implicate Order*. Bohm's book is not about religion. It is a discussion of the implications of the discoveries of physicists of our times. Bohm is considered one of the great physicists of the twentieth century.

In this book Harry says that he found a concept of

the "More" (although Bohm doesn't use that word) that provided an image that was profoundly satisfying to him—a confirmation of the existence of something that is beyond the world as we ordinarily experience it, yet that Harry, a longtime agnostic, could accept as real.

Harry says that now when he goes to church, he makes the words of prayers meaningful by thinking of God as the vast field of energy present everywhere, that links everything, that *is* everything, and yet is more than the things we see and touch. He thinks of God as the power and creativity inherent in everyone sitting in the pews around him, as well as the pews themselves, and the light streaming in from the windows. He thinks of God as the energy that brought us into being and keeps us alive.

At work, when things get rushed and pressure builds, Harry sometimes takes a break, closes the door to his office, and looks out the window for a moment. He takes a few long, deep breaths and reminds himself that everyone and every event he deals with is an expression of a larger, mysterious dimension: what Bohm refers to as the "implicate order" from which all things that exist in this world, Bohm's "explicate order," unfold. In other words, we are, literally, a projection of an immense, multidimensional greater reality. We are, as Harry puts it, "notes played by God."

Harry says that when he thinks of God and his life in this way it "rings true, and I can feel the presence of that deeper dimension coursing through all life and binding it together."

Esther

A Pattern for Comfort and Support

Esther also feels a presence, but a different one.

Esther has attended a conservative Baptist church her entire life. She is a mid-level hospital executive. She begins each day by reading her Bible, and she has read it through many times. Although she owns several translations, her favorite is the King James. She attends, and often leads, a Sunday morning Bible study at her Baptist church. She also makes a point of going to Wednesday night prayer meeting with her husband (her grown children are in other cities) and to the church supper that follows it.

Usually she is able to find time to pray at least once each day. Esther prays for her family, for her co-workers, for her city, for herself, for friends, for the underprivileged, and even for politicians. (She is not a member of any political party.) When she prays Esther often feels the presence of Jesus in the room. She says it is as if he were standing near her, caring for her, listening to her words, and also hearing the thoughts behind her words. She feels loved and protected by Jesus.

This pattern of church, Bible, and prayer has been a constant for her entire life. She recalls memorizing psalms as a child because her mother and grandmother expected her to do so. She attended church on Sundays and Wednesday nights as she grew up, and even while she was a college student. She met her husband at church, and he has attended with her throughout the length of their relationship.

Esther says that the comfort and support she has received from these lifelong practices is priceless.

A Sunday in September

I am alone at home with the dogs. I am thinking about God. There are so many ways people have thought about God: as the hidden intelligence behind all; as a cosmic force; as an old man in the sky; as Apollo; as the universal self; as the eternal present; as Jesus; as the Holy Spirit; as the milieu in which we live and move and have our being; as the still, small voice deep inside ourselves; as the underlying relationship that supports and ties together all relationships—relationships between people, between all creatures, between all things; as the mysterious power that drives all that is; as the present; and as the mystery.

I think: We did not create ourselves, nor did the rock outside my window, nor the tree beside it, nor the earth, nor the sun. These are hardly profound thoughts, but they are what I am thinking today.

I think: Some people believe that the universe

called itself into being. If so, then, for them, the creative power of the universe is ultimate. In that way of understanding God, everyone is a believer. And since no one can explain why there is anything at all, or answer any of hundreds of similar questions, it should be obvious that we spend each moment in an impenetrable mystery. The greatest mystery of all, the deepest, is here right before our noses, every second of every day. That force, that power, that mystery, that intelligence, by whatever name we choose, is revealed, expressed, and unfolded in all that is. The name doesn't matter and yet it does.

I consider that the necessary implication of this is that I ought to trust. I ought to do so completely, radically, without hesitation or reservation. After all, I owe my existence and every experience to this eternal, cosmic mystery, which I may, or may not, choose to call God. But I have a problem living that trust.

I tell myself that I believe that God is present in

everything life brings: the good and the bad. I believe that our lives are expressions of God, that we are always and everywhere in God. The trust I want is not passive. We are instruments of God. Thus, I ask myself, What is there to fear? We are part of and inseparable from God.

If only I could live it.

The Lord gives and the Lord takes away, blessed be the name of the Lord.

—Job 1:21

Luke
Fast Food, Slow Contemplation

Luke is around forty. Married, with two children. His wife teaches third grade. He works for a beer distributor. A few years ago a group of men at his Lutheran congregation attended a weekend retreat at a monastery near Kansas City. One of the brothers gave a talk about the process of *lectio divina:* the ancient technique of slow contemplative reading and praying the Bible.

As described by this monk, the first step of *lectio divina* is to find a passage of scripture that speaks to us in a personal way. The second step is to read it very slowly, listening attentively to hear what it might have to say to us today. The third step is to pray, understanding prayer to be a conversation with God in which God speaks to us through the scripture, and we speak to God, allowing the words we have been reading and pondering to touch us deeply. Then, we rest with the result.

Luke has been practicing *lectio divina* since the retreat. At first he found it difficult to find a place where he could do so without being interrupted or distracted. However, he began stopping at a fast food restaurant on his way to work. He carries his Bible in, gets a cup of coffee and something to eat, and sits by himself. There, between home and work, safe from interruption, he can settle in for twenty uninterrupted minutes.

Rebecca

Wordless Prayer

Rebecca is in her late forties. She was born, and still is, an Episcopalian. She lives on the East Coast and she fits the stereotype of her religion. She comes from an upper middle-class family, attended private schools, and is married to a successful businessman. She has one child at home, a son age seventeen, and another son who is a sophomore in college.

Sometime in her thirties she had a friend who suggested that she read a little quarterly publication, available at her church, called *Forward Day by Day*. It contains daily Bible readings and a short commentary on each of the readings. The authors who write the commentaries are anonymous. Rebecca began doing her spiritual reading each morning after the house emptied.

She says that after she started the practice of reading the daily Bible citations and the commentary, she began reading the Episcopal service of morning prayer. But after some time she gave up the practice of regularly reading the service, although she still goes back to it from time to time. She says that she found that the service had too many words, even though they were words that she loved and had heard many times since she was a young child. She felt that they were getting in her way. She says she loves her church, but it uses too many words. Now most mornings she doesn't read anything. She just sits with her hands folded in her lap. When she does that, is she praying?

"Does not effort mean a struggle to change what is into what is not, or into what it should be or should become? That is, we are constantly struggling to avoid facing what is, or we are trying to get away from it or to transform or modify what is.... The moment I accept what is there is no struggle.... Now if one does not make an effort to run away, what happens?... When we accept what is without avoidance, we will find that there comes a state of being in which all strife ceases."

—J. Krishnamurti

Ben

Thankfulness as Healing Prayer

Ben is an engineer. Although Ben is successful in his career and has a good marriage, throughout his life he has been plagued with depression. His is a mild depression, which comes and goes. Ben's recurring bouts of depression have, in his words, caused his life to be something less than it should have been.

Ben is Jewish, but he does not attend services. He is something of a student of theology. Ben believes in God, but he does not use that word. He believes that there is a creative force that is active in history.

Ben says that two years ago he made a change in his life that has paid dividends. The change was simply this:

He began making a mental list of things to be thankful for. When Ben makes his list of things to be thankful for in his car, he develops the list out loud.

Ben says that over the two years in which he has been following this practice, he can see a change in his life. Although he still has bouts of depression, the exercise of listing all of the matters for which he is thankful is an effective antidote.

Ben has a thirty-minute commute each day and he tries to start each day by making his list. Sometimes he forgets, but most days he thinks of it. He has a reminder built into Microsoft Outlook on his office computer. He has programmed the computer to ask him: "What are you thankful for today?"

When Ben is thankful, is he praying?

Alone with God, Nature, and City

P.K. is in his late seventies. A distinguished man, he dresses in a dark business suit and wears a carnation every day. He is the founder of a large accounting firm. P.K. is a lifelong bachelor and lives in a large apartment on the top floor of a downtown building. He has endowed a series of lectures at a local college. P.K. plans never to retire.

For over forty years, weather permitting, P.K. has walked to and from work. It is three miles each way. P.K. does not consider his walk to work as a spiritual practice, or even as a form of walking meditation, but it is. This is the time of day when he is alone with God, nature, and his city. He considers these three elements to be mutually supportive. He is aware of the sky, the weather, the trees, the seasons of the year, and the various businesses he passes on his route. His walk is brisk and he breathes deeply.

If you pass P.K. in your car you will see a man who is completely absorbed in the task at hand. If you observe him closely, you can see the ghost of smile on his face.

P.K. makes no attempt to discipline or guide his thoughts while he walks, but he finds that over the years he has developed a mental peace during the walk. Rarely does he think of the day's issues while he is walking. He makes no effort to pray, or to visualize, or to guide his thoughts in any way. He simply allows himself to be wherever he is during these walks.

Think that you're gliding out from
    the face of a cliff
like an eagle. Think you're walking
like a tiger walks by himself in the
    forest.

—Rumi

Andi

Perceiving the Cries
of the World

Andi is twenty-three years old. She was born and raised in a loosely Lutheran household in Colorado. She left the Lutheran Church at age thirteen, and over the next few years she became a student of Buddhism. When she was twenty-one she spent four months in Nepal experiencing Buddhist meditation. She now lives in Gunsan City, South Korea, where she teaches English and studies Buddhism and martial arts.

She says, "Some of the most passionate and loving people I know are Zen Masters, Tibetan lamas, Franciscan monks, and Lutheran laypeople, all of whom exemplify the compassion and wisdom I personally strive to bring to action in my life. What these people do differently from most people is that they direct their passion and love, helping other people and easing the suffering of the world."

Andi sets aside some time each day—sometimes more, sometimes less, but always some—for focused and deliberate spiritual practice. Each morning, she makes offerings of water and incense on her altar, and she makes three prostrations and recites the Four Great Vows: "Sentient beings are numberless, we vow to save them all; delusions are endless, we vow to cut through them all; the teachings are infinite, we vow to learn them all; the Buddha Way is inconceivable, we vow to attain it."

Most mornings she meditates for twenty to thirty minutes and chants for ten to fifteen minutes. When her knees aren't hurting she also does 108 bows. Once a week, she attends a service at her local temple, where she chants and bows with other laypeople and the nuns who run the temple. She also goes on short retreats about four times a year.

"Bowing is a very important part of my practice. I do say a mantra, usually 'Kwan Seum Bosal,' which is the name of the Bodhisattva of compassion in Korean. [Bodhisattva is a being on the path to awakening—a kind of Buddhist 'saint,' though this is an inadequate comparison.] I try to hold the Kwan Seum Bosal mantra at all times, even when I'm just walking. Kwan Seum Bosal means 'she who perceives the cries of the world.'"

The time Andi makes for sitting, chanting, and bowing sets the tone for her day. She thinks of formal practice as a warm-up for the challenges to come. It is also a time when she has a chance to "cultivate mindfulness in the rare quiet and solitude of the morning. It helps me act compassionately and mindfully during the rest of the day."

Andi says, "Really, when you're engaged in spiritual practice, there is no separation between formal practice and everyday life. Spiritual practice has given my life a direction: help stop suffering, help all sentient beings. It sounds real cheesy, but it isn't. It's hard work, and it's often frustrating as I deal with my own limitations and what seems like the endless suffering around me. Spiritual practice isn't about grand, sweeping changes wrought in an instant. Spiritual practice is the sweet maturation of human potential. It can take time, and it can happen in small increments. The wonder and the joy of spiritual practice come when I'm able to do the right thing at the right moment and *bam!* cut off suffering for myself and others.

"Practice is necessary. Daily practice and also more intense periods, like retreats, are the only way I've found to bring spirituality into action. My friends are all young, and I fight the tide of going to bars and staying out late because I know it'll mean I can't get up and meditate in the morning. But making that time and seeing it as something you give yourself is crucial. Spiritual practice is a gift. It helps me stay balanced. It allows me to breathe and focus."

Zach

Co-worker with God

Zach was trained as an accountant. After spending a decade working for an international company, he found himself in the Netherlands being offered a large promotion. His boss asked him, "What are your goals?" Zach says that it suddenly came to him that he wanted to be a healer. He turned down the promotion and returned to the United States to study. He became a neuromuscular therapist.

Today, twenty years later, Zach has a small office in a suburban office building. Just before he opened his practice, he and his wife went alone to the office and meditated there to fill the space with positive energy.

Zach was raised in the Greek Orthodox faith but he is now a member of Eckaankar, which, according to a pamphlet he gave me, is a "religion of the light and sound of God." Each member of Eckaankar considers himself or herself as a co-worker with God.

As Zach works on his patients each day, he uses his hands as the hands of God, and he seeks, through them, to heal.

A typical day of Zach's begins with early morning meditation. He sits in a quiet place, closes his eyes and relaxes, and then sings "Hu." The word is pronounced "hue." Hu is an ancient name for God.

Zach says that this daily practice opens his heart and helps him experience love, joy, and freedom. During the day as he works, Zach thinks of God and silently names God.

Edgar
Offering Compassion

Edgar lives in Texas and works for a dental supply company. He is an active volunteer for an organization that opposes the death penalty. He is a Unitarian who is intrigued with Buddhism.

Buddhist compassion, as Edgar tells it, has to do with regular practice, not with words and theories. He points out that every day provides us with numerous opportunities to be compassionate. Instead of resenting those who do harm, Edgar says, we must pity them for having lost the opportunity to live the rich, full life of those who live in compassion.

Each morning Edgar begins his day with meditation.

Usually his wife joins him. They light a candle and sit quietly together. During these times Edgar doesn't attempt to empty his mind. For years he tried to do so, and he eventually gave it up. Now he visualizes scenes. They are often based on his past, sometimes the recent past, sometimes from many years ago. In each scene he visualizes someone offering care and empathy to the others present. If he puts himself in the tableau, he imagines that he is the one offering compassion.

He says that this morning practice is similar to a warm-up before entering a game. Edgar practices "mindfulness" during the working day. He says that he repeatedly reminds himself that everyone with whom he comes in contact has a core nature that is just as pure as the nature of the Buddha, even though it may be buried in ignorance and fear. This is true for co-workers, friends, family, and even the criminals who have been given the death sentence.

James
Reminders in the Real World

James is a dentist. He has three grown sons and a daughter-in-law. He is Greek Orthodox. I asked him (while he was working on my teeth) whether he did anything to bring a spiritual dimension into his working day.

He said that in his faith, physical reminders are important. He told me that he wears a cross under his shirt where he can feel it on his chest. He pointed out that in his office there are several icons, some more subtle than others. In the room in which he was working on my teeth there is a fish tank. In the tank, in addition to the usual rocks and plastic vegetation, there is a small model of a church with an Orthodox cross on the steeple.

James said that throughout the day he says the Jesus prayer to himself silently: "Lord Jesus Christ, have mercy on me." Sometimes he shortens it to "Lord have mercy." Throughout the day he makes the sign of the cross. After an intense working period, when he comes up for air, he often stops and says a silent prayer.

James reports that after following this pattern for several years, there is a harmony to his day that would not otherwise exist.

Charles
Making the Mundane into the Holy

Charles is in his early fifties and is the editor of a major metropolitan newspaper. He is Jewish. He has two grown stepchildren and a wife who is employed in communications for another company.

I asked Charles what he does to bring a spiritual element into his life, and he said he was going to give me a very Jewish answer. He explained that, as a Jew, he did not separate his days into times when he is spiritual and times when he is not. He says that his goal as a practicing Jew is to make the mundane into the holy.

When Charles takes a break to have a cup of coffee, he says, "Bracha," which is a Hebrew prayer lasting about fifteen seconds and is an acknowledgment that God has brought him the coffee. Charles starts his day with a set of prayers that takes about five minutes and then he ends his day with another set of prayers lasting about the same amount of time. Charles says, "My goal is 24/7, but of course I do not accomplish that."

Charles is a member of a Reform Jewish congregation, but he subscribes to the Orthodox Jewish goal of making everything that one does holy by remembering God and the relationships God has commanded us to have. Charles attempts to fill every day with prayer: in the morning, at every meal, in the evening, and especially when anything good happens.

A Monday Evening in December

I am sitting in LaGuardia Airport waiting for my plane. Because I am at the Northwest gate used for departures to Memphis, I have seen three people I know. My business this morning was finished early, but I could not get on the 2:40 p.m. flight, so I am waiting for the 6:40 p.m. flight home (my original reservation).

I look around and think: so many people, so many cell phones (I have one, too). When I first visited New York over thirty years ago, I had the same thought as today: "So many people." How can there be anything significant about each of us? By the same reasoning I consider the uncountable stars and think: How can there be anything significant about the Earth, much less each person on it? Although the conclusion "insignificant" does not logically follow from the proposition "only one of billions," it seems to.

I look primarily at the women. Tall, short, fat, thin,

old, young, black, white, Hispanic. Many have shopping bags and books. There are a few red Christmas sweaters. I assume such sweaters are not worn by anyone from New York, only by women from the Midwest and the South.

Many people are reading, but most are simply waiting in a state of quiet—lives suspended, waiting to travel, waiting for home or business or vacation, waiting for the next destination. Some sleep or seem to, but there is an underlying state of awareness. We read, we watch each other, we listen to CNN, we eavesdrop on conversations, but we are ever alert for our boarding call.

Across the way there is a brunette woman with her husband, both just a few years younger than I am. From their clothes, luggage, books, and demeanor, I see that they are people of my class, education, income, and background. She has deep, dark eyes and a calm, pretty face. In another mixture of time and chance I could have gone to school with her, dated her, even married her or someone like her. Such is the way we make the connections that may last a lifetime.

Now I see the face of one of my daughter's friends, cell phone to ear, but I won't speak if she doesn't see me because I have forgotten her name. I imagine that if everyone waiting at LaGuardia Northwest gate nine for the plane to Memphis were to play the game "Who do we know in common?" ninety-five percent of us would have, at most, two degrees of separation. If we used shared institutions—colleges, churches, businesses —as denominators, we would find many of those in common, too. And, of course, all of us have bought the same brands of clothing, appliances, cars, and food—such commonality is too ubiquitous to have meaning. We have much more than that in common. Although I hate to think of it, now that we are in flu season, in the several hours I have been here, the air that has been in my lungs has also been in the lungs of many others.

Here are Christmas decorations. Here are polite, quiet people, and news on TV monitors. Is there God in this place? Here is a deep mystery. Here we all are.

What does it all mean? There were years when I believed that if I could not put the meaning of life into words, life must not have a meaning. Now I wonder why I ever thought that. Just because I can't put it into words doesn't mean that it has no meaning. This assembly of strangers and friends at the lobby at gate nine just *is,* and that trumps whatever words or thoughts I might have.

A Note about Finding Time

Not too long ago I gave a talk at an Episcopal church in Burlington, North Carolina. I said in that talk that performing a daily spiritual practice had increased the quality of my life. During the time for questions, a young mother said, "My life is already too full. How am I going to make the time?"

That is the problem of our era, isn't it?

My answer was, and is: don't. Don't "make" the time. Don't adopt a practice that you have to force into an already crowded day. Somehow we always find the time for that which we like doing. Each of us has the ability to find a spiritual practice (perhaps, if we are fortunate, more than one) that fits our nature so well that we will perform it because we want to. When we discover that, we won't carry it out because it leads to something else or because it makes us a better person; we will do it because it is an end in itself.

For twenty-five years I played tennis. I didn't have to force myself to play—I wanted to. At age fifty-one I found that I enjoyed golf more than tennis at that time in my life. I don't play golf, and I didn't play tennis, in order to improve myself. Playing was, and is, an end, not a means.

My grandmother tried to get me to read the Bible each day. It worked for her; it didn't for me. But thirty years later I started taking a few minutes each morning for some spiritual reading. I only read books that interested me. I look forward to those twenty to thirty minutes each morning even more than I do to playing golf.

I am told that daily life itself can be a spiritual practice if it is lived with the right openness to experience its magic. Of course, only saints manage that on a consistent basis. However, it isn't too much to hope that we can accomplish that for a few minutes from time to time. All we have to do is find the practices that bring us joy.

SUGGESTIONS FOR PRACTICE

Maura Shaw, who (you will recall from the introduction) is guilty of choosing me to write this book, thought it would be helpful to have a summary of the spiritual practices reported in this book as well as a few others: sort of a menu that one could select from. She not only suggested the idea, when I expressed some doubt about my ability to do this well, she was kind enough to assemble it. This was a gift to the reader and to me. She did a better job than I could have.

Spiritual Practice of Reading

e⌒ Every morning at breakfast, read a variety of spiritual writers from many different faith traditions, from ancient texts such as the Bhagavad Gita to more modern philosophers such as Paul Tillich. The list of suggested readings at the end of this book may give you some ideas of where to start. Many of these books are classics of spiritual writing and will be available in inexpensive editions or at your local library.

e⁓ If the start of the day at your house is somewhat rushed and noisy, consider leaving for work twenty minutes earlier than usual, to allow time for a quiet reading period at a coffee shop or fast-food restaurant on the way to your workplace.

e⁓ Many people find that reading the service of morning prayer from the Episcopal Book of Common Prayer starts their day off in a special way. Read aloud or read silently to yourself—whatever feels most comfortable to you. (And you don't need to be an Episcopalian to benefit from this practice.)

༄ Daily Bible readings are a way to enter sacred space each day. If a passage strikes a deep chord within you, take the time to memorize it and you'll have it available to you at any time of the day or night.

༄ The Book of Psalms has inspired, comforted, and encouraged people for thousands of years. The practice of reading and contemplating a psalm each day can lead to further spiritual engagement, as you carry the message of that particular psalm through your workday.

༄ Sometime during the day, take a spiritual nourishment break. Open your Bible or Qur'an or other sacred text to a page at random, place your index finger on the page, and read the passage underneath. You may be surprised to find yourself in a verse that you wouldn't deliberately turn to but that is relevant to your life today. God has a way of sending messages.

Spiritual Practice of Writing

e Daily journal writing has long been a spiritual practice of individuals in many different religious traditions, from monks (Christian, Buddhist, and Hindu) to mystics to poets. Read a scriptural text and then respond to its meaning in a personal journal. Write a poem or a prayer or a sentence or two.

e Bring thankfulness into your consciousness by writing a list of the blessings in your life. Maintain the list, add to it, and review it when you are feeling overwhelmed by the problems of the world. Or, review the list every day when you arrive at work, before you leave the car.

e Start a prayer journal, or even a list tucked into your daily planner, of all those people for whom you pray every day. The cofounder of the Catholic Worker movement, Dorothy Day, had a list with hundreds of names; your list may be shorter—but everyone is in need of prayer.

Spiritual Practice of Prayer

e⁓ If you like to focus your intentions by using a rosary or prayer beads, the commute to work on the train or bus may be just the right opportunity for you to start or end your workday with prayer. A shorter string of rosary beads, often called a Celtic rosary, is easy to tuck into a pocket.

e⁓ Praying when you first awake in the morning and before you go to sleep at night is a very personal way to keep a spiritual presence in your life, especially if you engage in spontaneous prayer as well as more formal prayers.

e⁓ Muslims pray five times a day to keep the presence of God always with them. It's a practice anyone can incorporate, though. Follow the cycle of the day by saying a short prayer upon rising, in the mid-morning, in the early afternoon, at the close of the workday, and before retiring at night.

e∿ When you're walking the dog in the quiet of early morning or late at night, find time for prayer as you stroll along holding the leash. A dog can be a loving companion on your spiritual journey.

e∿ When life is complicated and harried, you need only three prayers: Help, Forgive Me, and Thank You. Simply whisper them to God.

e∿ *Lectio divina* is a traditional practice in the Catholic Church but can be practiced by people of any faith. Read a passage of scripture, think about its deepest meaning, and pray for enlightenment as to its spiritual significance for you. Twenty minutes of quiet time spent in *lectio divina* can nourish your prayer life.

e∿ Sitting in silence with God is an easy practice to add to your daily routine. Perhaps you can take only a minute or two before getting out of the car when you arrive at your workplace—but those moments of silent communication with the Divine will center your day.

e~ Fill the day with small prayers. The Jewish tradition offers prayers for every daily activity, so that we can be present with God in every moment. No one has to know that you say a silent prayer whenever you pour a cup of coffee or press the button for the elevator.

Spiritual Practice of Meditation

e~ Morning and evening meditation can be done very effectively following yoga practice, when the body is relaxed and the mind is still. But if you don't have time for yoga, a simple relaxation of the muscles of your body will increase your ability to focus on a spiritual connection.

ᏋᎣ Meditating for twenty minutes twice daily can be done in a Christian form using the Jesus prayer or a mantra such as "Jesus, Abba." This inner-focused silent contemplation is called centering prayer.

ᏋᎣ If you can leave your workplace at lunchtime, pack or pick up a quick meal to eat and then spend the rest of the time in quiet meditation. You can drive to a nearby park or even meditate in your car.

ᏋᎣ Walking meditation is a practice recommended by the Buddhist teacher and monk Thich Nhat Hanh. Simply focus your mind on your breathing and walk peacefully on the earth—whether you're walking down a country lane or on a city sidewalk.

ᏋᎣ If you like to fish, the hours you spend in a boat or on the banks of a stream can provide a wonderful opportunity to be alone with God. On these excursions it doesn't matter whether you bring home fish or not. Your soul will be fed.

❧ Using a sacred word or a mantra as a focal point for meditation is very helpful. You might use a traditional "Om" or a simple word like "Peace" or a very short phrase such as "God is Love." Breathe in and out to the rhythm of the word.

❧ Acting with compassion and mindfulness during the whole day can be a form of meditation and active prayer.

Spiritual Practice of Physical Space

❧ Deep breathing can be used as a spiritual respite in the office. Feeling each breath you take, focusing on the physical gift of breathing and of life itself, can bring you closer to the ideal unity of body, mind, and spirit.

e⌒ Breathing in a conscious way can help you to feel the energy of God in the world, even when phones are ringing and machines are clacking away. At Thich Nhat Hanh's Buddhist retreat centers around the world, the staff members pause to take a deep calming breath whenever they hear a phone ring.

e⌒ You might like to create a sacred space for prayer at home or at the office, keeping physical reminders of spiritual connection in sight. Whether you call it a personal altar or a prayer corner, find a quiet place out of the traffic path to display whatever objects will remind you of the Divine being present in your life—seashells, fresh flowers, a favorite book of prayers, religious symbols or statues. A prayer corner in your workplace may need to be as simple and discreet as a polished stone inscribed with an inspirational word.

❧ Fasting to strengthen the spirit is a practice that many religious traditions use from time to time. If you are new to the practice of fasting, ask someone who has fasted how to go about it, or read a book written by a knowledgeable practitioner. You can observe a fast from all food for a day, or from meat, or even from a non-food form of sustenance, such as electricity. The sacrifice of the fast is intended to bring your attention to all that God provides for us.

Spiritual Practice of Music

❧ Take a little time out in the evening to light a candle and listen to music that connects you with the Divine. You might choose to listen to various chants—Hindu chants in Sanskrit, Gregorian chants in Latin, Taizé chants in English—or instrumental music such as Native American flutes or world music with drums and voice. Try gospel or traditional hymns, classical piano, operatic arias. Let your heart sing. If you don't have quiet time in the evening, listen to inspiring music while driving to work in the morning or on your way home at night.

e↝ If you sing or chant, your car is a perfect private venue. Sing while driving in traffic or while waiting in the parking lot. Sing along to a tape or CD that lifts up your spirit.

e↝ Sound vibration such as bells or singing bowls can give you the sensation of experiencing divine energy. Try combining sound with prayer. Ring bells or chimes before and after meditation.

Spiritual Practice of Community

e↝ Going on short retreats (a long weekend or even a day) is a good way to keep your spiritual life in tune. If it's possible to stay overnight at the retreat center, make plans to do so—you'll meet other people who are interested in spiritual development just as you are. Many retreat centers offer weekend workshops on meditation, prayer, sacred music, and other practices. You can also find places that offer personal retreats for going deep within.

৶ Making the effort to keep in close relationship with family and friends can be a form of spiritual practice. Visit an elderly relative, take a child for a walk and an ice cream cone, meet friends for coffee to share support and concern. The community of spirit is strengthened in many ordinary ways.

৶ Weekly or monthly meetings with a spiritual director can be of great help in following a spiritual path. Some individuals like to reach outside their own faith to work with a spiritual director of another faith tradition—broadening knowledge of others' beliefs can deepen the commitment to one's own.

ᴇ Attending daily Mass or another prayer service provides a way to keep in touch with spiritual practice every day of the week. Check to see if early morning or noontime services are available near your workplace.

ᴇ Joining a religious community as a lay member provides a meaningful connection for some people. The commitment often is limited to weekends, and the religious community offers wonderful resources for living a spiritual life.

ᴇ Weekly or monthly participation in a study and discussion group can stimulate the mind as well as deepen the spiritual life. Most churches, synagogues, mosques, and spiritual retreat centers offer such groups.

∼ Spending time helping people in need is an active way to bring God into your life through doing God's work. You don't necessarily have to chop vegetables at a soup kitchen—you might volunteer to repair an elderly neighbor's broken window screens, or spend Saturday mornings giving beginner golf lessons to an inner-city youth group.

∼ Participation in interfaith activities can be a satisfying way to reach out to others in the spiritual community. Discussion groups, art and music presentations, potluck dinners—there are any number of activities that can bring people of many faiths together.

∼ Contributing to charity and other worthy causes can be a quietly rewarding and meaningful way to support the spiritual community. Sharing what we have with others is one of the basic practices of a God-affirming life.

e∿ You may be in the position to demonstrate ethical behavior in the management and practice of business. Even if you're not the head of your company, you can help to create a business atmosphere where employees are valued and respected, and where ethical behavior is encouraged in every aspect of working with clients, customers, and suppliers. Since we spend so much of our lives at work, we can use those hours to everyone's benefit by making them count, spiritually.

ABOUT THE READING LIST

Many books have helped make my mornings into times of pleasure. I like books that explore the implications of this endless mystery in which we find ourselves. Some of the books I have read, at least in substantial part (I do not claim to have read every page of all of them), are listed below. My taste won't be yours, but a few might be of interest.

I do not accept the view that we can divorce what we believe about the nature of the physical world from what we believe about God. Although some people claim to be able to do so, the history of religion shows that this is not possible for most of us. (Think of the upheaval caused by the shift from a pre-

Copernican view of the universe to the post-Copernican, or of the effect of Newtonian physics, which led to the widespread belief that nothing was real except the apparently tangible, material world. And quantum physics and relativity are changing our perspectives again.) My reading has included a number of books about science and physics. Nobel Prize–winning physicist David Bohm's book *Wholeness and the Implicate Order* is not a religious book, but his discussion of what he calls the "implicate order" sounds much like the mysterious, transcendent dimension that has been called "the beyond in our midst" by the Protestant theologian Dietrich Bonhoeffer. Another physicist who has written a book which has unintended spiritual implications is Henry P. Stapp. I found his book *Mind, Matter, and Quantum Mechanics* particularly meaningful.

Also important to me have been books about Taoism, Hinduism, and Judaism. Every time I pick up the Taoist classics, the *Tao Te Ching* and the works of Chang Tzu, I feel that I have returned to a profoundly sane perspective. The Hindu philosopher Ecknath Easwaren has a gift for explanation of that religion, and he is an engaging and warm person who is worth reading even if one is not particularly interested in learning about his tradition. After you read him, you begin to understand how profound Hinduism can be. Some of the Jewish authors who have been important to me are Martin Buber, Abraham Joshua Heschel, and David Cooper.

A Christian theologian who has been significant to my life is Raimundo Panikkar. Panikkar is well known in Europe but not in America. His father was the Indian ambassador to Spain for Gandhi's government (and a Hindu), and his mother was a Spanish Roman Catholic. Panikkar is Roman Catholic. He holds graduate degrees in science, philosophy, and theology, and he communicates in eleven languages. He has written many books, but *The Silence of God: The Answer of the Buddha* is, in my opinion, his best.

In the introduction I have already mentioned Paul Tillich. I haven't tried to read his multi-volume *Systematic Theology,* but fortunately there are a number of shorter works that make him accessible. I believe that he is the most important Protestant theologian of the last century. Matthew Fox's *Passion for Creation: The Earth-Honoring Spirituality of Meister Eckhart* deserves to be a classic. Fox's translation of, and commentary on, the works of that seminal medieval Christian thinker shows how Christianity can be understood in a way that is consistent with all we have learned to date about the nature of the universe.

I have enjoyed every book Annie Dillard has written. Lucinda Vardey's collection of writings from all the major religious traditions, called *God in All Worlds,* is currently riding around in my car, and anytime I get stuck in traffic or waiting in line, I pick it up. I recommend Frederick

Buechner's non-fiction books. The last book I read before I turned in this manuscript was Karen Armstrong's spiritual autobiography, *The Spiral Staircase;* it was a knockout.

I could go on and on. For what it is worth, the following reading list contains many of the books I have enjoyed.

A Reading List

Armstrong, Karen. *The Spiral Staircase*. New York: Random House, 2004.

Barrow, John D. *The World within the World*. Oxford: Oxford University Press, 1988.

Bass, Diana Butler. *Strength for the Journey: A Pilgrimage of Faith in Community*. San Francisco: Jossey-Bass, 2002.

Bohm, David. *On Creativity*. London: Routledge, 1998.

———. *Wholeness and the Implicate Order*. London: Routledge & Kegan Paul, 1980.

Bonhoeffer, Dietrich. *Letters and Papers from Prison*. 3rd ed. New York: Macmillan, 1967.

Borg, Marcus J. *The God We Never Knew*. New York: HarperCollins, 1998.

Borg, Marcus J., ed. *God at 2000*. Harrisburg, PA: Morehouse Publishing, 2001.

Borg, Marcus J., and N. T. Wright. *The Meaning of Jesus: Two Visions*. San Francisco: HarperCollins, 1998.

Buber, Martin. *I and Thou*. New York: Charles Scribner's Sons, 1958.

———. *Moses: The Revelation and the Covenant*. New York: Harper & Row, 1958.

———. *Tales of the Hasidim*. New York: Schocken Books, 1947.

———. *The Way of Response,* edited by N. N. Glatzer. New York: Schocken Books, 1971.

Buechner, Frederick. *Telling Secrets*. San Francisco: HarperCollins, 1991.

Carter, Stephen L. *The Culture of Disbelief: How American Law and Politics Trivialize Religious Devotion*. New York: Anchor Books, 1994.

Carrigan, Henry L., Jr. ed. *The Way of Perfection: Saint Teresa of Avila.* Brewster, MA: Paraclete Press, 2000.

Chuang Tzu. *The Complete Works of Chuang Tzu,* edited by Burton Watson. New York: Columbia University Press, 1968.

Clayton, P. *God and Contemporary Science.* Edinburgh: Edinburgh University Press, 1997.

Cobb, John B. *Charles Hartshorne: The Einstein of Religious Thought, 1897–2000.* Claremont, CA: The Center for Process Studies, 2001.

Cooper, David A. *God Is a Verb: Kabbalah and the Practice of Mystical Judaism.* New York: Riverhead Books, 1997.

Cousins, Norman, comm. *Nobel Prize Conversations.* Dallas: Saybrook Publishing Company, 1985.

D'Aquili, Eugene, Vince Rause, and Andrew Newberg. *Why God Won't Go Away: Brain Science and the Biology of Belief.* New York: Ballantine Books, 2001.

Dennett, Daniel. *Consciousness Explained*. Boston: MIT Press, 1991.

Dillard, Annie. *For the Time Being*. New York: Alfred A. Knopf, 1999.

———. *Pilgrim at Tinker Creek*. New York: Harper & Row, 1974.

Dowell, Graham. *Enjoying the World: The Rediscovery of Thomas Traherne*. Harrisburg, PA: Morehouse, 1990.

Dyson, Freeman. *Infinite in All Directions* [Gifford Lectures]. New York: Harper & Row, 1988.

Easwaren, Eknath, trans. and comm. *The Bhagavad Gita*. New York: Vintage Books, 1985.

———. trans. and comm. *The Dhammapada*. Tomales, CA: Nilgiri Press, 1985.

Easwaren, Eknath. *The Bhagavad Gita for Daily Living*. 4 vols. Tomales, CA: Nilgiri Press, 1975.

Farrington, Debra K. *Living Faith Day by Day*. New York: Penguin Putman, 2000.

Feynman, Richard P. *The Pleasure of Finding Things Out*. Cambridge, MA: Perseus Publishing, 1999.

———. *Six Easy Pieces*. New York: Addison Wesley Publishing, 1995.

Fox, Matthew. *Passion for Creation: The Earth-Honoring Spirituality of Meister Eckhart*. Rochester, VT: Inner Traditions, 1991.

Furlong, Monica. *Contemplating Now*. Cambridge, MA: Cowley Publications, 1971.

———. *Merton: A Biography*. San Francisco: Harper & Row, 1985.

Gardner, Martin. *The Night Is Large*. New York: St. Martin's/Griffin, 1996.

Hammarskjøld, Dag. *Markings*. New York: Ballantine Books, 1964.

Hartshorne, Charles, and William L. Reese. *Philosophers Speak of God*. Chicago: University of Chicago Press, 1953.

Hayward, Jeremy W. *Perceiving Ordinary Magic:*

Science and Intuitive Wisdom. Boston: New Science Library, 1984.

Heschel, Abraham Joshua. *God in Search of Man: A Philosophy of Judaism*. New York: Farrar, Straus & Giroux, 1955.

James, William. *The Varieties of Religious Experience*. Introduction by Reinhold Neibuhr. New York: Simon and Schuster, 1997.

Jones, Roger S. *Physics as Metaphor*. New York: Meridian, 1982.

King, Ursula. *Christian Mystics*. Mahwah, NJ: Paulist Press, 2001.

Krishnamurti, J. *On God*. New York: HarperCollins, 1992.

———. *The First and Last Freedom*. New York: HarperCollins, 1954.

Leech, Kenneth. *Experiencing God: Theology as Spirituality*. New York: Harper & Row, 1985.

Main, John. *Moment of Christ*. New York: Crossroad, 1984.

Malin, Shimon. *Nature Loves to Hide: Quantum Physics and the Nature of Reality, A Western Perspective.* New York: Oxford University Press, 2001.

Matt, Daniel C. *The Essential Kabbalah: The Heart of Jewish Mysticism.* Edison, NJ: Castle Books, 1997.

McFague, Sallie. *Models of God.* Philadelphia: Fortress Press, 1987.

Mindell, Arnold. *Quantum Mind: The Edge between Physics and Psychology.* Portland, OR: Lao Tse Press, 2000.

Murchie, Guy. *The Seven Mysteries of Life: An Exploration in Science and Philosophy.* New York: Houghton Mifflin, 1978.

Nadeau, Robert, and Menas Kafatos. *The Conscious Universe.* New York: Springer Verlag, 2000.

———. *The Non-Local Universe.* New York: Oxford University Press, 1999.

Nasr, Seyyed Hossein. *Knowledge of the Sacred.* Albany: State University of New York Press, 1989.

Norris, Kathleen. *The Cloister Walk.* New York: Riverhead Books, 1996.

Pagels, Elaine. *Beyond Belief: The Secret Gospel of Thomas.* New York: Random House, 2003.

Pandita, Saydaw U. *In This Very Life: The Liberation Teachings of the Buddha.* Somerville, MA: Wisdom Publications, 1991.

Panikkar, Raimundo. *Invisible Harmony.* Minneapolis: Fortress Press, 1995.

———. *The Silence of God: The Answer of the Buddha.* Maryknoll, NY: Orbis Books, 1989.

———. *The Unknown Christ of Hinduism.* Maryknoll, NY: Orbis Books, 1981.

———. *The Vedic Experience.* New Delhi: Motilal Publishers, 1983.

Peacocke, A. R. *Creation and the World of Science.* Oxford: Oxford University Press, 1979.

Prigogine, Ilya, and Yves Elskens. "Irreversibility, Scholasticity and Non-locality in Classical Dynamics," in *Quantum Implications,* edited by Basil J. Hiley and F. David Peat. London: Routledge & Kegan Paul, 1987.

Sanford, John A. *The Kingdom Within.* New York: Paulist Press, 1970.

Shaw, Maura, and the Editors at SkyLight Paths. *Forty Days to Begin a Spiritual Life: Today's Most Inspiring Teachers Help You on Your Way.* Woodstock, VT: SkyLight Paths, 2002.

Spong, John Shelby. *Resurrection.* San Francisco: HarperCollins, 1994.

Stapp, Henry P. *Mind, Matter, and Quantum Mechanics.* Heidelberg: Springer Verlag, 1993.

Suchocki, Marjorie. *God Christ Church: A Practical Guide to Process Theology.* New York: Crossroad/Herder & Herder, 1990.

Suzuki, D. T. *Zen Buddhism*. New York: Doubleday Anchor, 1956.

Taylor, Brian C. *Becoming Christ: Transformation through Contemplation,* Cambridge, MA: Cowley Publications, 2002.

Teilhard de Chardin, Pierre. *The Divine Milieu*. New York: Harper & Row, 1960.

———. *The Heart of the Matter*. New York: Harcourt Brace Jovanovich, 1976.

Tickle, Phyllis, ed. *The Divine Hours*. 3 vols. New York: Doubleday, 2000–2001.

Tillich, Paul. *The Dynamics of Faith*. New York: Harper & Row, 1957.

———. *The Essential Tillich,* edited by E. Forrester Church. New York: Collier, 1987.

———. *The Eternal Now*. New York: Charles Scribner's Sons, 1963.

Tzu, Lao. *Tao Te Ching*, edited by Paul K. T. Sih. New York: St. John's University Press, 1961.

Underhill, Evelyn. *Mysticism: A Study in the Nature and Development of Man's Spiritual Consciousness*. New York: World, 1911.

Vardey, Lucinda, ed. *God in All Worlds*. New York: Pantheon, 1995.

Viney, Donald. *Charles Hartshorne and the Existence of God*. Albany: State University of New York Press, 1985.

Watts, Alan. *Behold the Spirit*. New York: Random House, 1947.

———. *The Wisdom of Insecurity*. New York: Random House, 1951.

Weiss, Paul. "The Living System," in *Beyond Reductionism: New Perspectives in the Life Sciences*, edited by A. Koestler and J. R. Smythies. Boston: Beacon, 1964.

Wilber, Ken, ed. *Quantum Questions*. Boulder, CO: New Science Library, 1984.

Wittgenstein, Ludwig. *Tractatus Logico-Philosophicus*. London: Routledge, 1981.

Yutang, Lin. *The Wisdom of Lao Tsu*. New York: Random House, 1948.

NOTES

1. *Atlantic Monthly,* January–February 2003, 42–3.

2. Paul Tillich, *The Eternal Now* (London: SCM Press, 1963), 71.

3. John Main, *Moment of Christ* (New York: Crossroad, 1984).

4. Martin Buber, *Moses: The Revelation and the Covenant* (New York: Harper & Row, 1958), 52.

5. Brian C. Taylor, *Becoming Christ* (Cambridge, MA: Cowley Publications, 2000), 220.

6. Graham Dowell, *Enjoying the World: The Rediscovery of Thomas Traherne* (Wilton, CT: Morehouse, 1990), 3.

Notes

Notes

Notes

Notes

Notes

Notes

About SKYLIGHT PATHS Publishing

SkyLight Paths Publishing is creating a place where people of different spiritual traditions come together for challenge and inspiration, a place where we can help each other understand the mystery that lies at the heart of our existence.

Through spirituality, our religious beliefs are increasingly becoming a part of our lives—rather than *apart* from our lives. While many of us may be more interested than ever in spiritual growth, we may be less firmly planted in traditional religion. Yet, we do want to deepen our relationship to the sacred, to learn from our own as well as from other faith traditions, and to practice in new ways.

SkyLight Paths sees both believers and seekers as a community that increasingly transcends traditional boundaries of religion and denomination—people wanting to learn from each other, *walking together, finding the way.*

Other Interesting Books—Spirituality

Lighting the Lamp of Wisdom: *A Week Inside a Yoga Ashram*
by *John Ittner*; Foreword by *Dr. David Frawley*

This insider's guide to Hindu spiritual life takes you into a typical week of retreat inside a yoga ashram to demystify the experience and show you what to expect from your own visit.
6 x 9, 192 pp, b/w photographs, Quality PB, ISBN 1-893361-52-7 **$15.95**;
HC, ISBN 1-893361-37-3 **$24.95**

Waking Up: *A Week Inside a Zen Monastery*
by *Jack Maguire*; Foreword by *John Daido Loori, Roshi*

An essential guide to what it's like to spend a week inside a Zen Buddhist monastery.
6 x 9, 224 pp, b/w photographs, Quality PB, ISBN 1-893361-55-1 **$16.95**;
HC, ISBN 1-893361-13-6 **$21.95**

Making a Heart for God: *A Week Inside a Catholic Monastery*
by *Dianne Aprile*; Foreword by *Brother Patrick Hart*, OCSO

This essential guide to experiencing life in a Catholic monastery takes you to the Abbey of Gethsemani—the Trappist monastery in Kentucky that was home to author Thomas Merton—to explore the details. "More balanced and informative than the popular *The Cloister Walk* by Kathleen Norris." —*Choice: Current Reviews for Academic Libraries*
6 x 9, 224 pp, b/w photographs, Quality PB, ISBN 1-893361-49-7 **$16.95**;
HC, ISBN 1-893361-14-4 **$21.95**

Come and Sit: *A Week Inside Meditation Centers*
by *Marcia Z. Nelson*; Foreword by *Wayne Teasdale*

Traveling through Buddhist, Hindu, Christian, Jewish, and Sufi traditions, this essential guide takes you to different meditation centers to meet the teachers and students and learn about the practices, demystifying the meditation experience.
6 x 9, 224 pp, b/w photographs, Quality PB, ISBN 1-893361-35-7 **$16.95**

Or phone, fax, mail or e-mail to: SKYLIGHT PATHS Publishing
Sunset Farm Offices, Route 4 • P.O. Box 237 • Woodstock, Vermont 05091
Tel: (802) 457-4000 • Fax: (802) 457-4004 • www.skylightpaths.com
Credit card orders: (800) 962-4544 (8:30AM–5:30PM ET Monday–Friday)
Generous discounts on quantity orders. SATISFACTION GUARANTEED. Prices subject to change.

Spiritual Biography

The Life of Evelyn Underhill
An Intimate Portrait of the Groundbreaking Author of Mysticism
by *Margaret Cropper*; Foreword by *Dana Greene*

Evelyn Underhill was a passionate writer and teacher who wrote elegantly on mysticism, worship, and devotional life. This is the story of how she made her way toward spiritual maturity, from her early days of agnosticism to the years when her influence was felt throughout the world.

6 x 9, 288 pp, 5 b/w photos, Quality PB, ISBN 1-893361-70-5 **$18.95**

Zen Effects: *The Life of Alan Watts*
by *Monica Furlong*

Through his widely popular books and lectures, Alan Watts (1915–1973) did more to introduce Eastern philosophy and religion to Western minds than any figure before or since. Here is the only biography of this charismatic figure, who served as Zen teacher, Anglican priest, lecturer, academic, entertainer, a leader of the San Francisco renaissance, and author of more than 30 books, including *The Way of Zen, Psychotherapy East and West* and *The Spirit of Zen*.

6 x 9, 264 pp, Quality PB, ISBN 1-893361-32-2 **$16.95**

Simone Weil: *A Modern Pilgrimage*
by *Robert Coles*

The French writer and philosopher Simone Weil (1906–1943) devoted her life to a search for God—while avoiding membership in organized religion. Robert Coles' intriguing study of Weil details her short, eventful life, and is an insightful portrait of the beloved and controversial thinker whose life and writings influenced many (from T. S. Eliot to Adrienne Rich to Albert Camus), and continue to inspire seekers everywhere.

6 x 9, 208 pp, Quality PB, ISBN 1-893361-34-9 **$16.95**

Mahatma Gandhi: *His Life and Ideas*
by *Charles F. Andrews*; Foreword by *Dr. Arun Gandhi*

Examines from a contemporary Christian activist's point of view the religious ideas and political dynamics that influenced the birth of the peaceful resistance movement, the primary tool that Gandhi and the people of his homeland would use to gain India its freedom from British rule. An ideal introduction to the life and life's work of this great spiritual leader.

6 x 9, 336 pp, 5 b/w photos, Quality PB, ISBN 1-893361-89-6 **$18.95**

Spiritual Practice

The Sacred Art of Bowing: *Preparing to Practice*
by *Andi Young*

This informative and inspiring introduction to bowing—and related spiritual practices—shows you how to do it, why it's done, and what spiritual benefits it has to offer. Incorporates interviews, personal stories, illustrations of bowing in practice, advice on how you can incorporate bowing into your daily life, and how bowing can deepen spiritual understanding.
5½ x 8½, 128 pp, b/w illus., Quality PB, ISBN 1-893361-82-9 **$14.95**

Praying with Our Hands: *Twenty-One Practices of Embodied Prayer from the World's Spiritual Traditions*
by *Jon M. Sweeney*; Photographs by *Jennifer J. Wilson;*
Foreword by *Mother Tessa Bielecki;* Afterword by *Taitetsu Unno, PhD*

This inspiring book of reflections and accompanying photographs shows us twenty-one simple ways of using our hands to speak to God, to enrich our devotion and ritual. All express the various approaches of the world's religious traditions to bringing the body into worship. Spiritual traditions represented include Anglican, Sufi, Zen, Roman Catholic, Yoga, Shaker, Hindu, Jewish, Pentecostal, Eastern Orthodox, and many others. 8 x 8, 96 pp, 22 duotone photographs, Quality PB, ISBN 1-893361-16-0 **$16.95**

The Sacred Art of Listening
Forty Reflections for Cultivating a Spiritual Practice
by *Kay Lindahl*; Illustrations by *Amy Schnapper*

More than ever before, we need to embrace the skills and practice of listening. You will learn to: Speak clearly from your heart • Communicate with courage and compassion • Heighten your awareness for deep listening • Enhance your ability to listen to people with different belief systems.
8 x 8, 160 pp, Illus., Quality PB, ISBN 1-893361-44-6 **$16.99**

Labyrinths from the Outside In
Walking to Spiritual Insight—A Beginner's Guide
by *Donna Schaper* and *Carole Ann Camp*

Labyrinth walking is a spiritual exercise *anyone* can do. This accessible guide unlocks the mysteries of the labyrinth for all of us, providing ideas for using the labyrinth walk for prayer, meditation, and celebrations to mark the most important moments in life. Includes instructions for making a labyrinth of your own and finding one in your area.
6 x 9, 208 pp, b/w illus. and photographs, Quality PB, ISBN 1-893361-18-7 **$16.95**

SkyLight Illuminations Series
Andrew Harvey, series editor

Offers today's spiritual seeker an enjoyable entry into the great classic texts of the world's spiritual traditions. Each classic is presented in an accessible translation, with facing pages of guided commentary from experts, giving you the keys you need to understand the history, context, and meaning of the text.

Bhagavad Gita: *Annotated & Explained*
Translation by *Shri Purohit Swami*; Annotation by *Kendra Crossen Burroughs*

"The very best Gita for first-time readers." —Ken Wilber

Millions of people turn daily to India's most beloved holy book, whose universal appeal has made it popular with non-Hindus and Hindus alike. This edition introduces you to the characters, explains references and philosophical terms, shares the interpretations of famous spiritual leaders and scholars, and more.
5½ x 8½, 192 pp, Quality PB, ISBN 1-893361-28-4 **$16.95**

The Way of a Pilgrim: *Annotated & Explained*
Translation and annotation by *Gleb Pokrovsky*

This classic of Russian spirituality is the delightful account of one man who sets out to learn the prayer of the heart—also known as the "Jesus prayer"—and how the practice transforms his life.
5½ x 8½, 160 pp, Illus., Quality PB, ISBN 1-893361-31-4 **$14.95**

The Gospel of Thomas: *Annotated & Explained*
Translation and annotation by *Stevan Davies*

Discovered in 1945, this collection of aphoristic sayings sheds new light on the origins of Christianity and the intriguing figure of Jesus, portraying the Kingdom of God as a present fact about the world, rather than a future promise or future threat. This edition guides you through the text with annotations that focus on the meaning of the sayings.
5½ x 8½, 192 pp, Quality PB, ISBN 1-893361-45-4 **$16.95**

Rumi and Islam: *Selections from His Stories, Poems, and Discourses—Annotated & Explained*
Translation and annotation by *Ibrahim Gamard*

Offers a new way of thinking about Rumi's poetry. Ibrahim Gamard focuses on Rumi's place within the Sufi tradition of Islam, providing you with insight into the mystical side of the religion—one that has love of God at its core and sublime wisdom teachings as its pathways.
5½ x 8½, 240 pp, Quality PB, ISBN 1-59473-002-4 **$15.99**

SkyLight Illuminations Series
Andrew Harvey, series editor

Zohar: *Annotated & Explained*
Translation and annotation by *Daniel C. Matt*

The best-selling author of *The Essential Kabbalah* brings together in one place the most important teachings of the *Zohar*, the canonical text of Jewish mystical tradition. Guides you step by step through the midrash, mystical fantasy, and Hebrew scripture that make up the *Zohar*, explaining the inner meanings in facing-page commentary. Ideal for readers without any prior knowledge of Jewish mysticism.
5½ x 8½, 176 pp, Quality PB, ISBN 1-893361-51-9 **$15.99**

Selections from the Gospel of Sri Ramakrishna
Annotated & Explained
Translation by *Swami Nikhilananda*; Annotation by *Kendra Crossen Burroughs*

Introduces the fascinating world of the Indian mystic and the universal appeal of his message that has inspired millions of devotees for more than a century. Selections from the original text and insightful yet unobtrusive commentary highlight the most important and inspirational teachings. Ideal for readers without any prior knowledge of Hinduism.
5½ x 8½, 240 pp, b/w photographs, Quality PB, ISBN 1-893361-46-2 **$16.95**

Dhammapada: *Annotated & Explained*
Translation by *Max Müller* and revised by *Jack Maguire*; Annotation by *Jack Maguire*

The Dhammapada—words spoken by the Buddha himself over 2,500 years ago—is notoriously difficult to understand for the first-time reader. Now you can experience it with understanding even if you have no previous knowledge of Buddhism. Enlightening facing-page commentary explains all the names, terms, and references, giving you deeper insight into the text.
5½ x 8½, 160 pp, b/w photographs, Quality PB, ISBN 1-893361-42-X **$14.95**

Hasidic Tales: *Annotated & Explained*
Translation and annotation by *Rabbi Rami Shapiro*

The allegorical quality of Hasidic tales can be perplexing. Here, they are presented as stories rather than parables, making them accessible and meaningful. Each demonstrates the spiritual power of unabashed joy, offers lessons for leading a holy life, and reminds us that the Divine can be found in the everyday. Annotations explain theological concepts, introduce major characters, and clarify references unfamiliar to most readers.
5½ x 8½, 240 pp, Quality PB, ISBN 1-893361-86-1 **$16.95**

Meditation/Prayer

Finding Grace at the Center: *The Beginning of Centering Prayer*
by *M. Basil Pennington, ocso, Thomas Keating, ocso,* and *Thomas E. Clarke, SJ*

The book that helped launch the Centering Prayer "movement." Explains the prayer of *The Cloud of Unknowing,* posture and relaxation, the three simple rules of centering prayer, and how to cultivate centering prayer throughout all aspects of your life.

5 x 7¼, 112 pp, HC, ISBN 1-893361-69-1 **$14.95**

Prayers to an Evolutionary God
by *William Cleary;* Afterword by *Diarmuid O'Murchu*

How is it possible to pray when God is dislocated from heaven, dispersed all around us, and more of a creative force than an all-knowing father? In this unique collection of eighty prose prayers and related commentary, William Cleary considers new ways of thinking about God and the world around us. Inspired by the spiritual and scientific teachings of Diarmuid O'Murchu and Teilhard de Chardin, Cleary reveals that religion and science can be combined to create an expanding view of the universe—an evolutionary faith.

6 x 9, 208 pp, HC, ISBN 1-59473-006-7 **$21.99**

Meditation without Gurus: *A Guide to the Heart of Practice*
by *Clark Strand*

Short, compelling reflections show you how to make meditation a part of your daily life, without the complication of gurus, mantras, retreats, or treks to distant mountains. This enlightening book strips the practice down to its essential heart—simplicity, lightness, and peace—showing you that the most important part of practice is not whether you can get in the full lotus position, but rather your ability to become fully present in the moment.

5½ x 8½, 192 pp, Quality PB, ISBN 1-893361-93-4 **$16.95**

Meditation & Its Practices: *A Definitive Guide to Techniques and Traditions of Meditation in Yoga and Vedanta*
by *Swami Adiswarananda*

Drawing on both classic and contemporary sources, this comprehensive sourcebook outlines the scientific, psychological, and spiritual elements of Yoga and Vedanta meditation.

6 x 9, 504 pp, HC, ISBN 1-893361-83-7 **$34.95**

Children's Spiritual Biography

MULTICULTURAL, NONDENOMINATIONAL, NONSECTARIAN

Ten Amazing People
And How They Changed the World
by *Maura D. Shaw*; Foreword by *Dr. Robert Coles*
Full-color illus. by *Stephen Marchesi*

For ages 7 & up

Black Elk • Dorothy Day • Malcolm X • Mahatma Gandhi •
Martin Luther King, Jr. • Mother Teresa • Janusz Korczak •
Desmond Tutu • Thich Nhat Hanh • Albert Schweitzer

This vivid, inspirational, and authoritative book will open new possibilities for children by telling the stories of how ten of the past century's greatest leaders changed the world in important ways.
8½ x 11, 48 pp, HC, Full-color illus., ISBN 1-893361-47-0 **$17.95**

Thich Nhat Hanh: *Buddhism in Action*
by *Maura D. Shaw*; Full-color illus. by *Stephen Marchesi*

For ages 7 & up

Warm illustrations, photos, age-appropriate activities, and Thich Nhat Hanh's own poems introduce a great man to children in a way they can understand and enjoy. Includes a list of important Buddhist words to know.
6¾ x 8¾, 32 pp, HC, Full-color illus., ISBN 1-893361-87-X **$12.95**

Gandhi: *India's Great Soul*
by *Maura D. Shaw*; Full-color illus. by *Stephen Marchesi*

For ages 7 & up

There are a number of biographies of Gandhi written for young readers, but this is the only one that balances a simple text with illustrations, photographs, and activities that encourage children and adults to talk about how to make changes happen without violence. Introduces children to important concepts of freedom, equality, and justice among people of all backgrounds and religions.
6¾ x 8¾, 32 pp, HC, Full-color illus., ISBN 1-893361-91-8 **$12.95**

Dorothy Day: *A Catholic Life of Action*
by *Maura D. Shaw*; Full-color illus. by *Stephen Marchesi*

For ages 7 & up

Introduces children to one of the most inspiring women of the twentieth century, a down-to-earth spiritual leader who saw the presence of God in every person she met. Includes practical activities, a timeline, and a list of important words to know.
6¾ x 8¾, 32 pp, HC, Full-color illus., ISBN 1-59473-011-3 **$12.99**